The Lion Children's
TREASURY
of
CLASSIC
VERSE

Compiled by David Self
Illustrated by Hannah Firmin

LION
Children's Books

For Robin

Compilation and introductions copyright © 2001 David Self
Illustrations copyright © 2001 Hannah Firmin
This edition copyright © 2001 Lion Publishing

The moral rights of the author and illustrator
have been asserted

Published by
Lion Publishing plc
Sandy Lane West, Oxford, England
www.lion-publishing.co.uk
ISBN 0 7459 3980 5

First edition 2001
1 3 5 7 9 10 8 6 4 2 0

Acknowledgments
Every effort has been made to trace and contact copyright owners.
We apologize for any inadvertent omissions or errors.
Extracts from the Authorized Version of the Bible (The King James Bible),
the rights in which are vested in the Crown, are reproduced
by permission of the Crown's Patentee, Cambridge University Press.
'Little Trotty Wagtail', 'Love Lies Beyond', 'St Martin's Eve',
'Pleasant Sounds' and 'Summer Moods' by John Clare
are reproduced with permission of Curtis Brown Ltd, London,
on behalf of Eric Robinson.
Copyright Eric Robinson 1984, 1967.

A catalogue record for this book is available
from the British Library

Typeset in 12/16 Latin 725 BT
Printed and bound in Spain

Contents

Introduction

These are some words which Christians sometimes say as a prayer:

Your presence, O Lord of light and love and power divine,
is always with me.
Because you are closer than breathing, I am able to talk
with you at all times and at any moment.

This book is a collection of poems which reminds us of that belief. God not only made the world and all that is in it such as the hills and the rivers, the sea, the plants, birds, animals and people. He is close to us at all times.

In compiling this book, I have chosen poems by the great or 'classic' poets who have written in the English language. I have not included writing by modern or living writers but have concentrated on those whose names are still famous even though they lived long ago. I have also included poems by some writers who are now less well known or who have become 'unfashionable' but who were once popular and deserve to be remembered.

Most of all, the anthology is meant to be a reminder of the ways poets have shown how important God is in this world: indeed, how close he is to his creation, closer even than breathing.

Note: *The explanations at the foot of each page are of words as they are used in those poems. Any cuts in poems are indicated by three dots, thus: …*

And God Made the World

Pippa, a young girl in a poem by Robert Browning, wakes early on a spring morning and sees God in everything around her – as does Emily Dickinson in all that happens to her each and every day. Believing that it is God who made the world, John Milton praises him for his creation in a version of Psalm 126.

Pippa's Song

The year's at the spring,
And day's at the morn;
Morning's at seven;
The hill-side's dew-pearled;
The lark's on the wing;
The snail's on the thorn;
God's in his heaven –
All's right with the world!

Robert Browning

The Only News I Know

The only news I know
Is bulletins all day
From Immortality.

The only shows I see,
To-morrow and To-day,
Perchance Eternity.

The only One I meet
Is God, – the only street,
Existence; this traversed

If other news there be,
Or admirabler show –
I'll tell it you.

Emily Dickinson

Perchance: perhaps

Praise the Lord

Let us with a gladsome mind
Praise the Lord, for he is kind,
For his mercies aye endure,
Ever faithful, ever sure.

Let us blaze his name abroad,
For of gods he is the God…

Who by his wisdom did create
The painted heav'ns so full of state.

Who did the solid Earth ordain
To rise above the watery plain…

And caused the golden-tressèd sun
All the day long his course to run.

The hornèd moon to shine by night
Amongst her spangled sisters bright…

All living creatures he doth feed
And with full hand supplies their need.

Let us therefore warble forth
His mighty majesty and worth.

That his mansion hath on high
Above the reach of mortal eye.
For his mercies aye endure,
Ever faithful, ever sure.

John Milton

Aye: *always.* **Ordain:** *order or command.*

Colours of Creation

For Christina Rossetti, the work of God is to be seen in the bright and bold colours of nature. Gerard Manley Hopkins sees his presence in the variety of softer colours also to be found in his creation.

Colours

What is pink?
　A rose is pink
　By the fountain's brink.

What is red?
　A poppy's red
　In its barley bed.

What is blue?
　The sky is blue
　Where the clouds float through.

What is white?
　A swan is white
　Sailing in the light.

What is yellow?
　Pears are yellow,
　Rich and ripe and mellow.

What is green?
　The grass is green
　With small flowers between.

What is violet?
　Clouds are violet
　In the summer twilight.

What is orange?
　Why, an orange,
　Just an orange!

Christina Rossetti

Pied Beauty

Glory be to God for dappled things –
   For skies of couple-colour as a brinded cow;
     For rose-moles all in stipple upon trout that swim;
Fresh-firecoal chestnut-falls; finches' wings;
   Landscape plotted and pieced – fold, fallow, and plough;
     And all trades, their gear and tackle and trim.

All things counter, original, spare, strange;
   Whatever is fickle, freckled (who knows how?)
     With swift, slow; sweet, sour; adazzle, dim;
He fathers-forth whose beauty is past change:
     Praise him.

Gerard Manley Hopkins

Dappled: marked with spots or patches of colour.
Brinded: streaked or spotted. Stipple: dots.

9

Every Living Creature

Many poets have written about the strangeness, the wonder and the variety of animals that God has made. William Blake in particular ponders how God came to make both a creature as gentle as a lamb and also the fierce tiger, while John Bunyan learns a lesson by watching a snail.

The Song of Creation

First He made the sun,
Then He made the moon,
Then He made a possum,
Then He made a coon.

Adam was the first man
The Lord put on the ground,
And mother Eve she was the one
Who made the good Lord frown.

All the other creatures
He made them one by one,
He stuck them on the fence to dry
As soon as they were done.

Author unknown

Possum: *opossum (small furry animal).*
Coon: *racoon (small tree-climbing animal).*

Little Lamb

Little Lamb, who made thee?
    Dost thou know who made thee?
Gave thee life, and bid thee feed
By the stream and o'er the mead;
Gave thee clothing of delight,
Softest clothing, woolly, bright;
Gave thee such a tender voice,
Making all the vales rejoice?
    Little Lamb, who made thee?
    Dost thou know who made thee?

    Little Lamb, I'll tell thee;
    Little Lamb, I'll tell thee:
He is called by thy name,
For he calls himself a lamb.
He is meek and he is mild,
He became a little child.
I a child, and thou a lamb,
We are called by his name.
    Little Lamb, God bless thee!
    Little Lamb, God bless thee!

William Blake

Mead: *meadow.*

The Tiger

Tiger, tiger, burning bright
In the forests of the night!
What immortal hand or eye
Could frame thy fearful symmetry?

In what distant deeps or skies
Burnt the fire of thine eyes?
On what wings dare he aspire?
What the hand dare seize the fire?

And what shoulder and what art
Could twist the sinews of thy heart?
And when thy heart began to beat,
What dread hand formed thy dread feet?

What the hammer, what the chain,
In what furnace was thy brain?
Did God smile his work to see?
Did He who made the lamb make thee?

William Blake

Symmetry: precise shape of its body.
Aspire: rise up.

Upon the Snail

She goes but softly, but she goeth sure;
    She stumbles not as stronger creatures do:
Her journey's shorter, so she may endure
    Better than they which do much further go.

She makes no noise, but stilly seizeth on
    The flower or herb appointed for her food,
The which she quietly doth feed upon,
    While others range, and gare, but find no good.

And though she doth but very softly go,
    However 'tis not fast, nor slow, but sure;
And certainly they that do travel so,
    The prize they do aim at, they do procure.

John Bunyan

Gare: stare about. Procure: achieve or reach.

Birds of the Air

Lord Tennyson pictures an owl watching what happens as night turns to morning (including the sails of a windmill starting to turn) – while John Clare's wagtail obviously enjoys a rainy day! Samuel Taylor Coleridge tells us what he thinks the birds are saying as they sing to one another all day long.

The Owl

When cats run home and light is come,
  And dew is cold upon the ground,
And the far-off stream is dumb,
  And the whirring sail goes round,
  And the whirring sail goes round;
    Alone and warming his five wits,
    The white owl in the belfry sits.

When merry milkmaids click the latch,
  And rarely smells the new-mown hay,
And the cock hath sung beneath the thatch
  Twice or thrice his roundelay,
  Twice or thrice his roundelay;
    Alone and warming his five wits,
    The white owl in the belfry sits.

Alfred Lord Tennyson

Rarely: remarkably well. Roundelay: song.

Little Trotty Wagtail

Little trotty wagtail, he went in the rain
And tittering tottering sideways, he ne'er got straight again.
He stooped to get a worm and looked up to catch a fly
And then he flew away ere his feathers they were dry.

Little trotty wagtail, he waddled in the mud
And left his little foot-marks, trample where he would.
He waddled in the water pudge and waggle went his tail
And chirruped up his wings to dry upon the garden rail.

Little trotty wagtail, you nimble all about
And in the dimpling water pudge you waddle in and out.
Your home is nigh at hand and in the warm pigsty,
So little Master Wagtail, I'll bid you a 'Goodbye'.

John Clare

Ne'er: never. **Pudge:** *little puddle.* **Nigh:** *near.*

Answer to a Child's Question

Do you ask what the birds say? The sparrow, the dove,
The linnet and thrush say, 'I love and I love!'
In the winter they're silent – the wind is so strong;
What it says I don't know, but it sings a loud song.
But green leaves and blossoms, and sunny warm weather,
And singing and loving – all come back together.
'I love and I love,' almost all the birds say,
From sun-rise to star-rise, so gladsome are they.
But the lark is so brimful of gladness and love,
The green field below him, the blue sky above,
That he sings and he sings, and for ever sings he –
'I love my love and my love loves me!'
'Tis no wonder that he's full of joy to the brim,
When he loves his love and his love loves him.

Samuel Taylor Coleridge

Lessons from the Leaves

It is a fact of nature that beautiful things do not last. As Robert Herrick notes, the blossom of a tree does not last for ever – but that does not stop the blossom being beautiful. It is also part of nature that, just as a rose has a beautiful flower, so it grows on a sharp bramble. Edmund Spenser suggests that all good things are accompanied by some drawbacks, and we should be willing to bear disadvantages so that we may enjoy the good things. In a similar way, Edward Thomas finds pleasure in a bed of stinging nettles!

To Blossoms

Fair pledges of a fruitful tree,
   Why do ye fall so fast?
   Your date is not so past;
But you may stay yet here a while
   To blush and gently smile,
     And go at last.

What, were ye born to be
   An hour or half's delight,
   And so to bid good-night?
'Twas pity Nature brought ye forth
   Merely to show your worth,
     And lose you quite.

But you are lovely leaves, where we
   May read how soon things have
   Their end, though ne'er so brave:
And after they have shown their pride
   Like you, a while: they glide
     Into the grave.

Robert Herrick

Pledges: *promises.*

14

Sweet is the Rose

Sweet is the rose, but grows upon a briar;
Sweet is the juniper, but sharp his bough;
Sweet is the eglantine, but pricketh near;
Sweet is the fir bloom, but his branches rough;
Sweet is the cypress, but his rind is tough;
Sweet is the nut, but bitter is his pill;
Sweet is the broom flower, but yet sour enough;
And sweet is moly, but his root is ill.
So every sweet with sour is tempered still,
That maketh it be coveted the more:
For easy things that may be got at will
Most sorts of men do set but little store.
Why then should I account of little pain,
That endless pleasure shall unto me gain?

Edmund Spenser

Eglantine: *sweet briar.* **Moly:** *plant with white flower and black root
(said to be magical).* **Coveted:** *envied.*

Tall Nettles

Tall nettles cover up, as they have done
These many springs, the rusty harrow, the plough
Long worn out, and the roller made of stone:
Only the elm butt tops the nettles now.

This corner of the farmyard I like most:
As well as any bloom upon a flower
I like the dust on the nettles, never lost
Except to prove the sweetness of a shower.

Edward Thomas

Butt: *stump.*

Nature's Song

Poets care about the sound of their poems when they are spoken aloud.
No wonder then that some (like Clare, Keats and Coleridge) have
written about the many different sounds of nature – sounds to be heard
not only in summer but also in winter.

Pleasant Sounds

The rustling of leaves under the feet in woods and
   under hedges;
The crumpling of cat-ice and snow down woodrides,
   narrow lanes and every street causeway;
Rustling through a wood or rather rushing, while the
   wind halloos in the oak-top like thunder;
The rustle of birds' wings startled from their nests or
   flying unseen into the bushes;
The whizzing of larger birds overheard in a wood,
   such as crows, puddocks, buzzards;

The trample of robins and woodlarks on the brown
   leaves, and the patter of squirrels on the green moss;
The fall of an acorn on the ground, the pattering of
   nuts on the hazel branches as they fall from ripeness;
The flirt of the ground-lark's wink from the stubbles –
   how sweet such pictures on dewy mornings, when
   the dew flashes from its brown feathers!

John Clare

Puddocks: *buzzards (a kind of bird).*

On the Grasshopper and Cricket

The poetry of earth is never dead:
   When all the birds are faint with the hot sun,
   And hide in cooling trees, a voice will run
From hedge to hedge about the new-mown mead.
That is the grasshopper's – he takes the lead
   In summer luxury; he has never done
   With his delights, for when tired out with fun,
He rests at ease beneath some pleasant weed.
The poetry of earth is ceasing never;
   On a lone winter evening, when the frost
   Has wrought a silence, from the stove there shrills
The cricket's song, in warmth increasing ever,
   And seems to one in drowsiness half lost
The grasshopper's among some grassy hills.

John Keats

Mead: *meadow.*

A Noise Like That

   A noise like that of a hidden brook
   In the leafy month of June,
   That to the sleeping woods all night
   Singeth a quiet tune.

Samuel Taylor Coleridge

Lazy Hazy Days of Summer

William Blake shows us that school children two hundred years ago were much like modern school children. They didn't always want to be in school on a fine summer's day! Michael Drayton and John Clare give us 'word pictures' of glorious moments from beautiful summer days.

from The School Boy

I love to rise in a summer morn,
When the birds sing on every tree;
The distant huntsman winds his horn,
And the skylark sings with me.
O! What sweet company.

But to go to school in a summer morn,
O! it drives all joy away;
Under a cruel eye outworn
The little ones spend the day
In sighing and dismay…

William Blake

*Winds: blows. **Cruel eye:** the teacher's gaze.*

Clear Had the Day Been

Clear had the day been from the dawn,
  All chequered was the sky,
Thin clouds, like scarves of cobweb lawn,
  Veiled heaven's most glorious eye.

The wind had no more strength than this,
  – That leisurely it blew –
To make one leaf the next to kiss
  That closely by it grew.

The rills, that on the pebbles played,
  Might now be heard at will;
This world the only music made,
  Else everything was still.

Michael Drayton

Rills: brooks.

Summer Moods

I love at eventide to walk alone
Down narrow lanes o'erhung with dewy thorn,
Where from the long grass underneath, the snail
Jet black creeps out and sprouts his timid horn.
I love to muse o'er meadows newly mown
Where withering grass perfumes the sultry air,
Where bees search round with sad and weary drone
In vain for flowers that bloomed but newly there,
While in the juicy corn the hidden quail
Cries 'wet my foot' and, hid as thoughts unborn.
The fairylike and seldom-seen landrail
Utters 'craik craik' like voices underground,
Right glad to meet the evening's dewy veil
And see the light fade into glooms around.

John Clare

Muse: think. Landrail: corncrake (a type of bird).

In Love with Night

We may think we prefer daytime to night-time but Lady Anne Lindsay's little poem neatly points out how necessary night-time is to the working of God's world. Meanwhile, the American poet Walt Whitman finds understanding not in a lecture given by a clever scientist but in looking up at the night sky. Two lines from a long poem called 'The Village Blacksmith' remind us how satisfying it is to go to bed after finishing a good day's work!

Day and Night

Said Day to Night,
'I bring God's light.
  What gift have you?'
  Night said, 'The dew.'

'I give bright hours,'
Quoth Day, 'and flowers.'
  Said Night, 'More blest,
  I bring sweet rest.'

Lady Anne Lindsay

Quoth: *said.*

When I Heard the Learn'd Astronomer

When I heard the learn'd astronomer,
When the proofs, the figures, were ranged in columns
   before me,
When I was shown the charts and diagrams, to add,
   divide, and measure them,
When I sitting heard the astronomer where he lectured
   with much applause in the lecture-room,
How soon unaccountable I became tired and sick,
Till rising and gliding out I wander'd off by myself,
In the mystical moist night-air, and from time to time,
Look'd up in perfect silence at the stars.

Walt Whitman

Learn'd (or learned): *having much knowledge.*

from The Village Blacksmith

Something attempted, something done,
Has earned a night's repose.

Henry Wadsworth Longfellow

Repose: *rest.*

Different Kinds of Good Weather

Too often (like Thomas Hardy) we think of wet weather as 'bad' weather and say we prefer spring to autumn. A famous painter called John Ruskin (who lived from 1819 to 1900) once said, 'There is really no such thing as bad weather; only different kinds of good weather.' That is what Sara Coleridge is celebrating in her poem about the months of the year.

Weathers

This is the weather the cuckoo likes,
   And so do I;
When showers betumble the chestnut spikes,
   And nestlings fly;
And the little brown nightingale bills his best,
And they sit outside at 'The Travellers' Rest',
And maids come forth sprig-muslin drest,
And citizens dream of the south and west,
   And so do I.

This is the weather the shepherd shuns,
   And so do I.
When beeches drip in browns and duns,
   And thresh, and ply;
And hill-hid tides throb, throe on throe,
And meadow rivulets overflow,
And drops on gate-bars hang in a row,
And rooks in families homeward go,
   And so do I.

Thomas Hardy

Betumble: shake. Spikes: flowers (of the chestnut tree). Bills: sings. Sprig-muslin: cotton embroidered with flower-designs. South and west: parts of England visited by holiday makers. Duns: dull colours. Thresh, and ply: toss and bend. Hill-hid tides: the sea, beyond the mountains. Throe: crash (of waves).

The Months of the Year

January brings the snow;
Makes the toes and fingers glow.

February brings the rain,
Thaws the frozen ponds again.

March brings breezes loud and shrill,
Stirs the dancing daffodil.

April brings the primrose sweet,
Scatters daisies at our feet.

May brings flocks of pretty lambs,
Skipping by their fleecy dams.

June brings tulips, lilies, roses;
Fills the children's hands with posies.

Hot July brings cooling showers,
Strawberries and gilly-flowers.

August brings the sheaves of corn,
Then the Harvest home is borne.

Warm September brings the fruit,
Sportsmen then begin to shoot.

Fresh October brings the pheasant;
Then to gather nuts is pleasant.

Dull November brings the blast,
Then the leaves are falling fast.

Chill December brings the sleet,
Blazing fire and Christmas treat.

Sara Coleridge

Fleecy: white and fluffy. Dams: mothers. Posies: small bunches of flowers. Gilly-flowers: scented flowers.

Harvest Days

In one way, autumn seems to be an ending but (as John Keats points out)
it is also a time of richness and harvest and has its 'music' just like spring.
Edward Thomas, too, finds joy in the scents of autumn as he digs his garden. And,
as Christina Rossetti reminds us, although harvest is an ending, we know that it
will be followed by spring-time – which brings new life and new growth.

To Autumn

Season of mists and mellow fruitfulness!
  Close bosom-friend of the maturing sun;
Conspiring with him how to load and bless
  With fruit the vines that round the thatch-
    eaves run;
To bend with apples the mossed cottage-trees,
  And fill all fruit with ripeness to the core;
    To swell the gourd, and plump the hazel
      shells
With a sweet kernel; to set budding more,
  And still more, later flowers for the bees,
  Until they think warm days will never cease,
    For Summer has o'er-brimmed their
      clammy cells.

Who hath not seen thee oft amid thy store?
  Sometimes whoever seeks abroad may find
Thee sitting careless on a granary floor,
  Thy hair soft-lifted by the winnowing wind;
Or on a half-reaped furrow sound asleep,
  Drowsed with the fume of poppies, while
    thy hook
    Spares the next swath and all its twined
      flowers;
And sometime like a gleaner thou dost keep
  Steady thy laden head across a brook;
  Or by a cider-press, with patient look,
    Thou watchest the last oozings, hours by
      hours.

Where are the songs of Spring? Ay, where are
    they?
  Think not of them, thou hast thy music too,
While barred clouds bloom the soft-dying day,
  And touch the stubble-plains with rosy hue;
Then in a wailful choir, the small gnats mourn
  Among the river sallows, borne aloft
    Or sinking as the light wind lives or dies;
And full-grown lambs loud bleat from hilly
    bourn;
  Hedge-crickets sing; and now with treble soft
  The redbreast whistles from a garden-croft,
    And gathering swallows twitter in the
      skies.

John Keats

Conspiring: plotting. Thatch-eaves: eaves of thatched cottages. Kernel: the inside of a nut. Winnowing: separating. Swath: row of corn. Stubble-plains: fields from which the corn has been harvested. Sallows: willow trees.

Digging

Today I think
Only with scents, – scents dead leaves yield,
And bracken, and wild carrot's seed,
And the square mustard field;

Odours that rise
When the spade wounds the root of tree,
Rose, currant, raspberry, or goutweed,
Rhubarb or celery;

The smoke's smell, too,
Flowing from where a bonfire burns
The dead, the waste, the dangerous,
And all to sweetness turns.

It is enough
To smell, to crumble the dark earth,
While the robin sings over again
Sad songs of Autumn mirth.

Edward Thomas

Amen

It is over. What is over?
  Nay, now much is over truly! –
Harvest days we toiled to sow for;
  Now the sheaves are gathered newly,
  Now the wheat is garnered duly.

It is finished. What is finished?
  Much is finished known or unknown:
Lives are finished; time diminished;
  Was the fallow field left unsown?
  Will these buds be always unblown?

It suffices. What suffices?
  All suffices reckoned rightly:
Spring shall bloom where now the ice is,
Roses make the bramble sightly,
  And the quickening sun shine brightly,
  And the latter wind blow lightly,
And my garden teem with spices.

Christina Rossetti

Suffices: *is enough.* **Sightly:** *good to look at.*
Quickening: *giving life.*

Wildness and Wet

For Thomas Hood the month of November means 'nothing': just gloom!
On the other hand, John Clare finds joy in a November evening spent at
home (St Martin's Eve falls on November 10th). Out of doors, Gerald Manley
Hopkins celebrates the 'wildness and wet' of God's creation – especially as
it is seen in a stream (or burn) tumbling down a hillside.

No!
(also known as November in England)

No sun – no moon!
No morn – no noon –
No dawn – no dusk – no proper time of day –
No sky – no earthly view –
No distance looking blue –
No road – no street – no 't'other side the way' –
No end to any Row –
No indications where the Crescents go –
No top to any steeple –
No recognitions of familiar people –
No courtesies for showing 'em –
No knowing 'em! –
No travelling at all – no locomotion,
No inkling of the way – no notion –
'No go' – by land or ocean –
No mail – no post –
No news from any foreign coast –
No Park – no Ring – no afternoon gentility –
No company – no nobility –
No warmth, no cheerfulness, no healthful ease,
No comfortable feel in any member –
No shade, no shine, no butterflies, no bees,
No fruits, no flowers, no leaves, no birds –
November!

Thomas Hood

No end to any Row: *no street end could be seen in the fog.*
Locomotion: *transport.* **Ring:** *pathway in a park.*

from St Martin's Eve

… The children hastening in from threatening rain
No longer round the fields for wild fruit run
But at their homes from morn to night remain
And wish in vain to see the welcome sun.
Winter's imprisonment is all begun
Yet when the wind grows troubleous and high,
Pining for freedom like a lovesick nun,
Around the garden's little bounds they fly
Beneath the roaring trees fallen apples to espy.

But spite of all the melancholy moods
That out of doors poor pleasure's heart alarms –
Flood bellowing rivers and wind roaring woods –
The fireside evening owns increasing charms;
What with the tale and eldern wine that warms
In purple bubbles by the blazing fire…

John Clare

Roaring trees: *trees through which the wind is roaring.* **Espy:** *spy.*
Tale: *conversation, stories.* **Eldern:** *mature, good to drink.*

Inversnaid

This darksome burn, horseback brown,
His rollrock highroad roaring down,
In coop and in comb the fleece of his foam
Flutes and low to the lake falls home.

A windpuff-bonnet of fawn-froth
Turns and twindles over the broth
Of a pool so pitchblack, fell-frowning,
It rounds and rounds Despair to drowning.

Degged with dew, dappled with dew
Are the groins of the braes that the brook
  treads through,
Wiry heathpacks, flitches of fern,
And the beadbonny ash that sits over the burn.

What would the world be, once bereft
Of wet and of wildness? Let them be left,
O let them be left, wildness and wet;
Long live the weeds and the wilderness yet.

Gerard Manley Hopkins

Burn: *mountain stream.* **Rollrock:** *tumbling pebbles and stones.*
Coop: *place where the water is 'cooped up' before overflowing.*
Degged: *sprinkled.* **Heathpacks:** *heather.* **Flitches:** *tufts.* **Bereft:** *robbed.*
(Some of the other words in 'Inversnaid' are the poet's own.)

27

Winter Weather

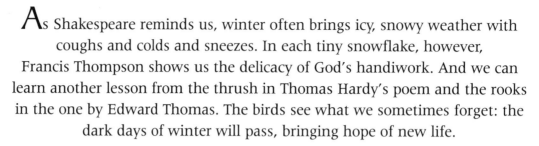

As Shakespeare reminds us, winter often brings icy, snowy weather with coughs and colds and sneezes. In each tiny snowflake, however, Francis Thompson shows us the delicacy of God's handiwork. And we can learn another lesson from the thrush in Thomas Hardy's poem and the rooks in the one by Edward Thomas. The birds see what we sometimes forget: the dark days of winter will pass, bringing hope of new life.

Winter

When icicles hang by the wall,
  And Dick the shepherd blows his nail,
And Tom bears logs into the hall,
  And milk comes frozen home in pail;
When blood is nipp'd and ways be foul,
Then nightly sings the staring owl,
    To-whit! To-who!
    A merry note,
While greasy Joan doth keel the pot.

When all aloud the wind doth blow,
  And coughing drowns the parson's saw;
And birds sit brooding in the snow,
  And Marian's nose looks red and raw;
When roasted crabs hiss in the bowl,
Then nightly sings the staring owl,
    To-whit! To-who!
    A merry note,
While greasy Joan doth keel the pot.

William Shakespeare

Blows his nail: blows on his fingers (to warm them).
Keel: stir or pour. Saw: sermon. Crabs: crab apples.

To a Snow-flake

What heart could have thought you? –
Past our devisal
(O filigree petal!)
Fashioned so purely,
Fragilely, surely,
From what Paradisal
Imagineless metal,
Too costly for cost?
Who hammered you, wrought you,
From argentine vapour? –
'God was my shaper.
Passing surmisal,
He hammered, He wrought me,
From curled silver vapour,
To lust of His mind: –
Thou could'st not have thought me!
So purely, so palely,
Tinily, surely,
Mightily, frailly,
Insculped and embossed,
With His hammer of wind,
And His graver of frost.'

Francis Thompson

Filigree: delicate. Argentine: silver. Surmisal: imagination.
Graver: engraver, shaper.

The Darkling Thrush

I leant upon a coppice gate
  When Frost was spectre-grey,
And Winter's dregs made desolate
  The weakening eye of day.
The tangled bine-stems scored the sky
  Like strings of broken lyres,
And all mankind that haunted nigh
  Had sought their household fires.

The land's sharp features seemed to be
  The century's corpse outleant,
His crypt the cloudy canopy,
  The wind his death-lament.
The ancient pulse of germ and birth
  Was shrunken hard and dry,
And every spirit upon earth
  Seemed fervourless as I.

At once a voice arose among
  The bleak twigs overhead
In a full-hearted evensong
  Of joy illimited;
An aged thrush, frail, gaunt, and small,
  In blast-beruffled plume,
Had chosen thus to fling his soul
  Upon the growing gloom.

So little cause for carolings
  Of such ecstatic sound
Was written on terrestrial things
  Afar or nigh around,
That I could think there trembled through
  His happy good-night air
Some blessed Hope, whereof he knew
  And I was unaware.

Thomas Hardy

*Coppice: small wood. **Eye of day:** sun. **Bine-stems:** bare stems of climbing plants. **Century's corpse:** Hardy wrote this poem on the last day of 1900. **Ecstatic:** very joyful. **Terrestrial:** earthly.*

Thaw

Over the land freckled with snow half-thawed
The speculating rooks at their nests cawed
And saw from elm-tops, delicate as flower of grass,
  What we below could not see, Winter pass.

Edward Thomas

Songs of Praise

Folliott Pierpoint praises God and gives him thanks for all that he has created in
a poem that has become a well-known hymn. William Wordsworth sees the
glorious work of God in the centre of London just as much as in the countryside.
Walt Whitman sees the same miracle in New York's Manhattan, in the countryside
or when meeting friends and also when watching bees, animals and birds.
Christina Rossetti praises God for the way that life can grow from a seed or an egg.

For the Beauty of the Earth

For the beauty of the earth,
For the beauty of the skies,
For the love which from our birth
Over and around us lies,
Christ, our God, to Thee we raise
This our sacrifice of praise.

For the beauty of each hour
Of the day and of the night,
Hill and vale and tree and flower,
Sun and moon and stars of light,
Christ, our God, to Thee we raise
This our sacrifice of praise…

For the joy of human love,
Brother, sister, parent, child,
Friends on earth and friends above,
For all gentle thoughts and mild,
Christ, our God, to Thee we raise
This our sacrifice of praise.

For each perfect gift of Thine
To our race so freely given,
Graces human and divine,
Flowers of earth and buds of heaven,
Christ, our God, to Thee we raise
This our sacrifice of praise…

Folliott Pierpoint

Sacrifice: offering.

Upon Westminster Bridge
3 September 1802

Earth has not anything to show more fair:
Dull would he be of soul who could pass by
A sight so touching in its majesty:
This city now doth, like a garment, wear
The beauty of the morning: silent, bare,
Ships, towers, domes, theatres, and temples lie
Open unto the fields, and to the sky;
All bright and glittering in the smokeless air.
Never did sun more beautifully steep
In his first splendour valley, rock, or hill;
Ne'er saw I, never felt, a calm so deep!
The river glideth at his own sweet will:
Dear God! The very houses seem asleep;
And all that mighty heart is lying still!

William Wordsworth

Steep: soak.

from Miracles

Why, who makes much of a miracle?
As to me I know of nothing else but miracles.
Whether I walk in the streets of Manhattan,
Or dart my sight over the roofs of houses towards the sky,
Or wade with naked feet along the beach just in the edge
   of the water,
Or stand under trees in the woods,
Or talk by day with anyone I love, or sleep in the bed at
   night with anyone I love,
Or sit at table at dinner with the rest,
Or look at strangers opposite me riding in the car,
Or watch honey-bees busy round the hive of a summer
   forenoon,
Or animals feeding in the fields,
Or birds, or the wonderfulness of insects in the air,
Or the wonderfulness of the sundown, or of stars shining
   so quiet and bright,
Or the exquisite delicate thin curve of the new moon in
   spring;
These with the rest, one and all, are to me miracles…

Walt Whitman

Judge Not According
to the Appearance

Lord, purge our eyes to see
Within the seed a tree,
   Within the glowing egg a bird,
    Within the shroud a butterfly;

Till taught by such, we see
Beyond all creatures Thee,
   And hearken for Thy tender word,
    And hear it, 'Fear not: it is I.'

Christina Rossetti

Purge: *cleanse.* ***Shroud:*** *cloak or (here) chrysalis.*

Early Days

One of the miracles of life is the birth of a baby. William Blake describes the happiness and also the tears of a new-born child. Robert Louis Stephenson gives advice to older children about growing up!

Infant Joy

'I have no name:
I am but two days old.'
What shall I call thee?
'I happy am,
Joy is my name.'
Sweet joy befall thee!

Pretty joy!
Sweet joy but two days old,
Sweet joy I call thee:
Thou dost smile,
I sing the while,
Sweet joy befall thee!

William Blake

Infant Sorrow

My mother groan'd, my father wept,
Into the dangerous world I leapt;
Helpless, naked, piping loud,
Like a fiend hid in a cloud.

Struggling in my father's hands,
Striving against my swaddling bands,
Bound and weary, I thought best
To sulk upon my mother's breast.

William Blake

Swaddling-bands: clothes like narrow lengths of bandages, once wrapped round babies.

Good and Bad Children

Children, you are very little
And your bones are very brittle;
If you would grow great and stately,
You must try to walk sedately.

You must still be bright and quiet,
And content with simple diet;
And remain, through all bewild'ring,
Innocent and honest children.

Happy hearts and happy faces,
Happy play in grassy places –
That was how, in ancient ages,
Children grew to kings and sages.

But the unkind and the unruly,
And the sort who eat unduly,
They must never hope for glory –
Theirs is quite a different story!

Cruel children, crying babies,
All grow up as geese and gabies,
Hated, as their age increases,
By their nephews and their nieces.

Robert Louis Stevenson

Sages: *wise people.* **Gabies:** *simpletons.*

Part of the Plan

Ella Wheeler Wilcox believes each one of us is part of God's plan for this world; and even if we do not understand that plan, it's up to us to make that plan work. Ben Jonson has the same idea. Each of us, in our own small way, can do something to make life better – even perfect! George Herbert simply praises God for making him as he is. (The original spelling of his poem has been kept to show how he makes his poem rhyme by dropping a single letter at a time.)

I Am

I know not whence I came,
   I know not whither I go;
But the fact stands clear that I am here
   In this world of pleasure and woe.
And out of the mist and murk
   Another truth stands plain:
It is my power, each day and hour,
   To add to its joy or pain.

I know that the earth exists,
   It is none of my business why;
I cannot find out what it's all about,
   I would but waste time to try.
My life is a brief, brief thing,
   I am here for a little space;
And while I stay I would like, if I may,
   To brighten and better the place.

The trouble, I think, with us all
   Is the lack of a high conceit.
If each man thought he was sent to this spot
   To make it a bit more sweet
How soon we could gladden the world,
   How easily right all wrong,
If nobody shirked, and each one worked
   To help his fellows along!

Cease wondering why you came,
   Stop looking for faults and flaws;
Rise up today in your pride and say:
   'I am part of the First Great Cause!
However full the world,
   There is room for an earnest man.
It had need of me, or I would not be:
   I am here to strengthen the plan.'

Ella Wheeler Wilcox

High conceit: *great imagination, great idea.*
First Great Cause: *the purpose of creation.*

Short Measures

It is not growing like a tree
  In bulk, doth make men better be;
Or standing long – an oak, three hundred year –
To fall a log at last, dry, bald, and sere:
    A lily of a day
    Is fairer far in May
  Although it fall and die that night;
  It was the plant and flower of light.
In small proportions we just beauties see;
And in short measures life may perfect be.

Ben Jonson

Paradise

I bless thee, Lord, because I GROW
Among the trees, which in a ROW
To thee both fruit and order OW.

What open force, or hidden CHARM
Can blast my fruit, or bring me HARM,
While the inclosure is thine ARM:

Inclose me still for fear I START;
Be to me rather sharp and TART,
Than let me want thy hand and ART.

When thou dost greater judgements SPARE,
And with thy knife but prune and PARE,
Even fruitful trees more fruitful ARE:

Such sharpness shows the sweetest FREND
Such cuttings rather heal than REND,
And such beginning touch their END.

George Herbert

Tart: *strict.* **Pare:** *trim, prune.* **Rend:** *tear (into pieces).*

Learning from Life

Isaac Watts thinks that the way a bee keeps busy every hour of the day can be a lesson to us all. We should learn not to be idle but to use our time as sensibly as that bee! Ella Wheeler Wilcox takes the idea a step forward: each one of us can do something each day to make the world a better place. George Herbert hopes that we can turn the routine jobs of daily life into a way of praising God. (In olden times, people thought there was an elixir or kind of liquid that would turn ordinary metal into gold.)

How Doth the Little Busy Bee

How doth the little busy bee
  Improve each shining hour,
And gather honey all the day
  From every opening flower!

How skilfully she builds her cells!
  How neat she spreads the wax!
And labours hard to store it well
  With the sweet food she makes.

In works of labour or of skill,
  I would be busy too;
For Satan finds some mischief still
  For idle hands to do.

In books, or work, or healthful play,
  Let my first years be passed,
That I may give for every day
  Some good account at last.

Isaac Watts

Today

Let me today do something that shall take
   A little sadness from the world's vast store,
And may I be so favoured as to make
   Of joy's too scanty sum a little more.

Let me not hurt by any selfish deed,
   Or thoughtless word, the heart of foe or friend,
Nor would I pass, unseeing, worthy need,
   Or sin by silence where I should defend.

However meagre be my worldly wealth,
   Let me give something that shall aid my kind –
A word of courage, or a thought of health,
   Dropped as I pass for troubled hearts to find.

Let me tonight look back across the span
   'Twixt dawn and dark, and to my conscience
      say:
'Because of some good act to beast or man
   the world is better that I lived today.'

Ella Wheeler Wilcox

My kind: my fellow human beings.

The Elixir

Teach me, my God and King,
   In all things thee to see,
And what I do in anything
   To do it as for thee;

   Not rudely, as a beast,
   To run into an action;
But still to make thee prepossest,
   And give it his perfection.

   A man that looks on glass,
   On it may stay his eye;
Or, if he pleaseth, through it pass,
   And then the Heaven espy.

   All may of thee partake:
   Nothing can be so mean,
Which with his tincture, (for thy sake)
   Will not grow bright and clean.

   A servant with this clause
   Makes drudgery divine;
Who sweeps a room, as for thy laws,
   Makes that and the action fine.

   This is the famous stone
   That turneth all to gold;
For that which God doth touch and own
   Cannot for less be told.

George Herbert

Rudely: roughly. **To make thee prepossest:** *to put God first.*
Espy: spy. **Tincture:** *'elixir' (God's 'magical medicine').* **The famous**
stone: *in olden times there was also thought to be a famous stone that*
would turn things into gold. **That which God doth touch and own:**
what God touches and makes his. **Cannot for less be told:** *cannot be*
valued less.

Best Behaviour

Robert Louis Stevenson's short rhyme is reminder of what makes 'good manners' while Jonathan Swift gives advice on the sort of manners or behaviour that will help us to remain friends with other people. The Ten Commandments are God's way of telling us how to behave. An unknown poet re-wrote them in this rhyming version.

Whole Duty of Children

A child should always say what's true,
And speak when he is spoken to,
And behave mannerly at table:
At least as far as he is able.

Robert Louis Stevenson

The Ten Commandments

1. Have thou no other gods but me,
2. And to no image bow thy knee.
3. Take not the name of God in vain:
4. The sabbath day do not profane.
5. Honour thy father and mother too;
6. And see that thou no murder do.
7. Abstain from words and deeds unclean;
8. Nor steal, though thou art poor and mean.
9. Bear not false witness, shun that blot;
10. What is thy neighbour's covet not.

These laws, O Lord, write in my heart, that I,
May in thy faithful service live and die.

Author unknown (1731)

Profane: treat with contempt. Abstain from: do not use.
Bear not false witness: do not lie. Covet: envy.

Twelve Articles
(from Daphne)

1. Lest it may more quarrels breed
   I will never hear you read.
2. By disputing I will never
   To convince you, once endeavour.
3. When a paradox you stick to,
   I will never contradict you.
4. When I talk, and you are heedless,
   I will show no anger needless.
5. When your speeches are absurd,
   I will ne'er object a word.
6. When you furious argue wrong,
   I will grieve, and hold my tongue.
7. Not a jest or humorous story
   Will I ever tell before ye:
   To be chidden for explaining
   When you quite mistake the meaning.
8. Never more will I suppose
   You can taste my verse or prose:
9. You no more at me shall fret,
   While I teach, and you forget;
10. You shall never hear me thunder,
    When you blunder on, and blunder.
11. Show your poverty of spirit,
    And in dress place all your merit;
    Give yourself ten thousand airs;
    That with me shall break no squares.
12. Never will I give advice
    Till you please to ask me thrice;
    Which if you in scorn reject,
    'Twill be just as I expect.

    Thus we both shall have our ends,
    And continue special friends.

Jonathan Swift

Disputing: arguing. Endeavour: try. Paradox: contradiction.
Chidden: told off. In dress place all your merit: think only
of your clothes. Break no squares: make no difference.

Life's Journey

Many writers have described life on this earth as a journey – a journey from birth, through childhood, then on to being an adult and finally to a resting place. This journey (Bunyan calls it a pilgrimage) may not always be easy. The important thing is to try to remain cheerful, to keep travelling and to accept what comes.

The Vagabond

Give to me the life I love,
    Let the lave go by me,
Give the jolly heaven above
    And the byway nigh me.
Bed in the bush with stars to see,
    Bread I dip in the river –
    There's the life for a man like me,
There's the life for ever.

Let the blow fall soon or late,
    Let what will be o'er me;
Give the face of earth around
    And the road before me.
Wealth I seek not, hope nor love,
    Nor a friend to know me;
All I seek, the heaven above
    And the road below me.

Or let autumn fall on me
    Where afield I linger,
Silencing the bird on tree,
    Biting the blue finger.
White as meal the frosty field –
    Warm the fireside haven –
Not to autumn will I yield,
    Not to winter even!

Let the blow fall soon or late,
    Let what will be o'er me;
Give the face of earth around
    And the road before me.
Wealth I ask not, hope nor love,
    Nor a friend to know me;
All I ask, the heaven above
    And the road below me.

Robert Louis Stevenson

Vagabond: *wanderer or tramp.* **Lave:** *remainder, other things.*

Jog on, Jog on

Jog on, jog on, the foot-path way,
    And merrily hent the stile-a:
A merry heart goes all the day,
    Your sad tires in a mile-a.

William Shakespeare

Hent: *take hold of.*

To Be a Pilgrim

Who would true valour see,
    Let him come hither:
One here will constant be,
    Come wind, come weather.
There's no discouragement
Shall make him once relent
His first avowed intent
    To be a pilgrim.

Who so beset him round
    With dismal stories,
Do but themselves confound, –
    His strength the more is;
No lion can him fright,
He'll with a giant fight;
But he will have a right
    To be a pilgrim.

Hobgoblin nor foul fiend
    Can daunt his spirit;
He knows he at the end
    Shall life inherit.
Then fancies flee away,
He'll fear not what men say;
He'll labour night and day
    To be a pilgrim.

John Bunyan

Avowed: *declared.* **Confound:** *confuse.*
Shall life inherit: *will gain everlasting life.*
Fancies: *delusions, imaginary worries*

Bad Lads and Lazy Lads

John Keats writes about himself running away – and finding everything just the same as it had been where he lived. Isaac Watts' poem is another warning: if we become lazy (a 'sluggard' is a lazy person), we shall find that things go wrong around us and we shall end up wasting our lives.

A Naughty Boy
(from A Song about Myself)

There was a naughty boy,
    And a naughty boy was he,
He ran away to Scotland,
    The people there to see –
    Then he found
    That the ground
    Was as hard,
    That a yard
    Was as long,
    That a song
    Was as merry,
    That a cherry
    Was as red,
    That lead
    Was as weighty,
    That fourscore
    Was as eighty,
    That a door
    Was as wooden
    As in England –
So he stood in his shoes
    And he wondered,
    He wondered,
He stood in his shoes
    And he wondered.

John Keats

Yard: a measure of distance (a little less than a metre). ***Fourscore:*** *four times twenty.*

The Sluggard

'Tis the voice of the sluggard; I hear him complain,
'You have waked me too soon; I must slumber again.'
  As the door on its hinges, so he on his bed,
  Turns his sides, and his shoulders, and his heavy head.

'A little more sleep, and a little more slumber' –
Thus he wastes half his days, and his hours without number;
  And when he gets up, he sits folding his hands,
  Or walks about saunt'ring, or trifling he stands.

I passed by his garden, and saw the wild brier,
The thorn and the thistle grow broader and higher.
  The clothes that hang on him are turning to rags;
  And his money still wastes till he starves or he begs.

I made him a visit, still hoping to find
He had took better care for improving his mind.
  He told me his dreams, talked of eating and drinking,
  But he scarce reads his Bible, and never loves thinking.

Said I then to my heart: 'Here's a lesson for me;
That man's but a picture of what I might be;
  But thanks to my friends for their care in my breeding,
  Who taught me betimes to love working and reading.'

Isaac Watts

Sluggard: lazy person. **Slumber:** *sleep.*

43

On the Road

What are now known as spirituals come from the churches where black Americans worshipped in the 1800s. Many began as 'song-sermons'. The preacher would sing his message and the congregation would then sing it back to him. One of these is 'Nobody Knows the Trouble I've Seen'. Robert Herrick's short poem reminds us to be cheerful whatever problems we meet, while another unknown poet writes about the troubles and dangers we meet as we go through life. In this poem, a child stands up to the devil – and frightens off the devil!

Nobody Knows the Trouble I've Seen

Nobody knows the trouble I've seen,
Nobody knows but Jesus;
Nobody knows the trouble I've seen,
Glory hallelujah!

Sometimes I'm up, sometimes I'm down,
O yes, Lord.
Sometimes I'm nearly to the ground,
O yes, Lord.

O nobody knows the trouble I've seen,
Nobody knows but Jesus;
Nobody knows the trouble I've seen,
Glory hallelujah!

Author unknown

Welcome What Comes

Whatever comes, let's be content withall:
Among God's blessings, there is no one small.

Robert Herrick

44

Meet-on-the-Road

'Now, pray, where are you going?' said Meet-on-the-Road.
'To school, sir, to school sir,' said Child-as-it-Stood.

'What have you in your basket, child?' said Meet-on-the-Road.
'My dinner, sir, my dinner sir,' said Child-as-it-Stood.

'What have you for dinner, child?' said Meet-on-the-Road.
'Some pudding, sir, some pudding, sir,' said Child-as-it-Stood.

'Oh, then I pray, give me a share,' said Meet-on-the-Road.
'I've little enough for myself, sir,' said Child-as-it-Stood.

'What have you got that cloak on for?' said Meet-on-the-Road.
'To keep the wind and cold from me,' said Child-as-it-Stood.

'I wish the wind would blow through you,' said Meet-on-the-Road.
'Oh, what a wish! What a wish!' said Child-as-it-Stood.

'Pray what are those bells ringing for?' said Meet-on-the-Road.
'To ring bad spirits home again,' said Child-as-it-Stood.

'Oh, then I must be going, child!' said Meet-on-the-Road.
'So fare you well, so fare you well,' said Child-as-it-Stood.

Author unknown

All Shall Be Free

Those of us who live in 'free' countries can easily take our freedom for granted. In America, it was only after the Civil War (1861–65), that slavery was finally abolished in the southern states. That war was fought partly to bring freedom to slaves and Julia Ward Howe's 'battle hymn' written in 1862 was the great song of the freedom fighters. John Barbour's poem reminds us of the value of freedom, while Sir Henry Wotton teaches us that true freedom means not being controlled by others; nor by our passions or tempers; nor by envy, rumours or fears.

Battle-Hymn of the Republic

Mine eyes have seen the glory of the coming of the Lord:
He is trampling out the vintage where the grapes of wrath are stored;
He hath loosed the fateful lightning of His terrible swift sword:
    His truth is marching on.

I have seen Him in the watch-fires of a hundred circling camps;
They have builded Him an altar in the evening dews and damps;
I can read His righteous sentence by the dim and flaring lamps:
    His day is marching on.

I have read a fiery gospel writ in burnished rows of steel:
'As ye deal with my contemners so with you My grace shall deal;
Let the Hero, born of woman, crush the serpent with His heel,
    Since God is marching on.'

He hath sounded forth the trumpet that shall never call retreat;
He is sifting out the hearts of men before His judgement-seat:
Oh, be swift, my soul, to answer Him! Be jubilant, my feet!
    Our God is marching on.

In the beauty of the lilies Christ was born across the sea,
With a glory in His bosom that transfigures you and me:
As He died to make men holy, let us die to make men free!
    While God is marching on.

Julia Ward Howe

Burnished: *polished.* **My contemners:** *people who scorn me.* **Hero:** *Jesus.*

from Robert the Bruce to His Army

… Ah! Freedom is a noble thing!
Freedom makes man to have liking:
Freedom all solace to man gives:
He lives at ease that freely lives!
A noble heart may have none ease,
Nor nothing else that may him please
If freedom fail…

John Barbour

Solace: peace of mind. **None ease:** *no rest.*

The Character of a Happy Life

How happy is he born and taught
That serveth not another's will;
Whose armour is his honest thought
And simple truth his utmost skill!

Whose passions not his masters are,
Whose soul is still prepared for death,
Not tied unto the world with care
Of public fame, or private breath;

Who envies none that chance doth raise,
Nor vice; who never understood
How deepest wounds are given by praise;
Nor rules of state, but rules of good:

Who hath his life from rumours freed,
Whose conscience is his strong retreat;
Whose state can neither flatterers feed,
Nor ruin make oppressors great;

Who God doth late and early pray
More of his grace than gifts to lend;
And entertains the harmless day
With a well-chosen book or friend;

– This man is freed from servile bands
Of hope to rise, or fear to fall;
Lord of himself, though not of lands;
And, having nothing, yet hath all.

Sir Henry Wotton

Chance: luck. **Servile:** *slave-like.*

The Pity of War

War brings great misery and much suffering. Yet sometimes it seems the only way to stop even greater evil. Even when that is the case, a war still seems far removed from what God wants for his world. Poets writing during World War One can remind us of the agony of that war – or as Wilfred Owen put it, 'the pity of war'. 'Futility' is about one particular soldier who has been killed.

Exposure

Our brains ache, in the merciless iced east winds that knive us…
Wearied we keep awake because the night is silent…
Low, drooping flares confuse our memory of the salient…
Worried by silence, sentries whisper, curious, nervous,
   But nothing happens.

Watching, we hear the mad gusts tugging on the wire,
Like twitching agonies of men among its brambles.
Northward incessantly, the flickering gunnery rumbles,
Far off, like a dull rumour of some other war.
   What are we doing here?

The poignant misery of dawn begins to grow…
We only know war lasts, rain soaks, and clouds sag stormy.
Dawn massing in the east her melancholy army
Attacks once more in ranks on shivering ranks of gray,
   But nothing happens.

Sudden successive flights of bullets streak the silence.
Less deathly than the air that shudders black with snow,
With sidelong flowing flakes that flock, pause, and renew;
We watch them wandering up and down the wind's nonchalance,
   But nothing happens.

Pale flakes with fingering stealth come feeling for our faces.
We cringe in holes, back on forgotten dreams, and stare, snow-dazed,
Deep into grassier ditches. So we drowse, sun-dozed,
Littered with blossoms trickling where the blackbird fusses.
   Is it that we are dying?

Slowly our ghosts drag home: glimpsing the sunk fires, glozed
With crusted dark-red jewels; crickets jingle there;
For hours the innocent mice rejoice: the house is theirs;
Shutters and doors, all closed: on us the doors are closed, –
    We turn back to our dying.

Since we believe not otherwise can kind fires burn;
Nor ever suns smile true on child, or field, or fruit.
For God's invincible spring our love is made afraid;
Therefore, not loath, we lie out here; therefore were born,
    For love of God seems dying.

To-night, His frost will fasten on this mud and us,
Shrivelling many hands, puckering foreheads crisp.
The burying-party, picks and shovels in their shaking grasp,
Pause over half-known faces. All their eyes are ice,
    But nothing happens.

Wilfred Owen

Salient: point in the defences. **Brambles:** *the knots on the barbed wire.*
Nonchalance: lack of concern. **Glozed:** *covered.*

Futility

Move him into the sun –
Gently its touch awoke him once,
At home, whispering of fields unsown.
Always it woke him, even in France,
Until this morning and this snow.
If anything might rouse him now
The kind old sun will know.

Think how it wakes the seeds, –
Woke, once, the clays of a cold star.
Are limbs, so dear-achieved, are sides,
Full-nerved – still warm – too hard to stir?
Was it for this the clay grew tall?
– O what made fatuous sunbeams toil
To break earth's sleep at all?

Wilfred Owen

Futility: pointlessness. **The clays:** *a poetic way of saying 'men'. (The Book of Genesis
says humans were created by God from the earth - or clay.)* **Cold star:** *the planet Earth.*

Simple Pleasures

How many times have you been told 'Remember to say thank you' when you have been given something – or when someone has done something for you? All Christians need to be reminded to say thank you to God for the everyday blessings he provides. This is what Robert Herrick is doing when he thanks God for his house and everything in it. First, however, John Bunyan shows the importance of being content with whatever God provides.

The Shepherd Boy's Song

He that is down needs fear no fall,
    He that is low, no pride;
He that is humble ever shall
    Have God to be his guide.

I am content with what I have,
    Little be it or much:
And, Lord, contentment still I crave;
    Because Thou savest such.

Fullness to such a burden is
    That go on pilgrimage;
Here little, and hereafter bliss,
    Is best from age to age.

John Bunyan

Crave: beg.

A Thanksgiving to God for His House

Lord, Thou hast given me a cell
  Wherein to dwell;
A little house, whose humble roof
  Is weather-proof;
Under the spars of which I lie
  Both soft and dry;
Where Thou my chamber for to ward
  Hast set a Guard
Of harmless thoughts, to watch and keep
  Me, while I sleep.

Low is my porch, as is my Fate,
  Both void of state;
And yet the threshold of my door
  Is worn by the poor,
Who thither come and freely get
  Good words, or meat:

Like as my parlour, so my hall
  And kitchen's small:
A little buttery, and therein
  A little bin,
Which keeps my little loaf of bread
  Unchipped, unflayed.

Some brittle sticks of thorn or briar
  Make me a fire,
Close by whose living coal I sit,
  And glow like it.

Lord, I confess too, when I dine,
  The pulse is thine,
And all those other bits that be
  There placed by Thee;
The worts, the purslane, and the mess
  Of watercress,
Which of Thy kindness Thou hast sent;
  And my content
Makes those and my beloved beet,
  To be more sweet.

'Tis Thou that crown'st my glittering
  hearth
  With guiltless mirth;
And giv'st me wassail bowls to drink,
  Spiced to the brink.
Lord, 'tis thy plenty-dropping hand,
  That soils my land,
And giv'st me, for my bushel sown,
  Twice ten for one.

Thou mak'st my teaming hen to lay
  Her egg each day:
Besides, my healthful ewes to bear
  Me twins each year;
The while the conduits of my kine
  Run cream (for wine).

All those and better Thou dost send
  Me, to this end,
That I should render, for my part,
  A thankful heart;
Which, fired with incense, I resign
  As wholly thine;
But the acceptance, that must be,
  My Christ, by Thee.

Robert Herrick

Cell: *one-room dwelling.* **Spars:** *rafters.* **Buttery:** *storeplace for food and drink.* **Unchipped, unflayed:** *unbroken (not nibbled by mice, etc.).* **Pulse:** *beans and lentils (cheap food).* **Worts:** *vegetables.* **Purslane:** *a herb.* **Mess:** *a serving.* **Wassail:** *drink.* **Bushel:** *a quantity of seed.* **Kine:** *cattle.*

Safe in God's Love

The Lady Julian, a nun who lived in Norwich, once had a dream or vision in which she saw a small object in her hand. It taught her three things. The same ideas (that God made, loves and looks after his world) are expressed in the American song 'He's Got the Whole World, in His Hand'.

He Keeps All That Is Made

He showed me a little thing, the size of a hazelnut,
  in the palm of my hand.
It was as round as a ball.
I looked at it with my mind's eye and I thought,
  'What can this be?'
And answer came, 'It is all that is made.'
I marvelled that it could last, for I thought it might
  have crumbled to nothing, it was so small.
And the answer came into my mind, 'It lasts and
  ever shall because God loves it.'

And all things have being through the love of God.

In this little thing I saw three truths.
  The first is that God made it.
  The second is that God loves it.
  The third is that God looks after it.

What is he indeed that is maker and lover and
  keeper?
I cannot find words to tell.
For until I am one with him,
I can never have true rest not peace.
I can never know it until I am held so close to him
  that there is nothing in between.

The Lady Julian of Norwich

52

He's Got the Whole World, in His Hand

Chorus:

He's got the whole world, in His hand,
He's got the whole wide world, in His hand,
He's got the whole world, in His hand,
He's got the whole world in His hand.

He's got the wind and the rain, in His hand,
He's got the wind and the rain, in His hand,
He's got the wind and the rain, in His hand,
He's got the whole world in His hand.
Chorus

He's got the sun and the moon, in His hand,
He's got the sun and the moon, in His hand,
He's got the sun and the moon, in His hand,
He's got the whole world in His hand.
Chorus

He's got the plants and the creatures, in His hand,
He's got the plants and the creatures, in His hand,
He's got the plants and the creatures, in His hand,
He's got the whole world in His hand.
Chorus

He's got everybody here, in His hand,
He's got everybody here, in His hand,
He's got everybody here, in His hand,
He's got the whole world in His hand.
Chorus

Author unknown

Fear No Evil

The Book of Psalms in the Bible is perhaps the greatest collection of religious poems. Their wording is especially beautiful in the English 1611 King James (or Authorized) translation of the Bible – and Psalm 23 is probably the best known of them all. Several poets, such as George Herbert, have written their own versions of it. The message of many of the Psalms is that, however difficult things seem to get, God will help those who ask his help.

The Lord is My Shepherd

The Lord is my shepherd; I shall not want.
He maketh me to lie down in green pastures:
He leadeth me beside the still waters.
He restoreth my soul:
He leadeth me in the paths of righteousness for his name's sake.
Yea, though I walk through the valley of the shadow of death,
I will fear no evil: for thou art with me; thy rod and thy staff they comfort me.
Thou preparest a table before me in the presence of mine enemies:
Thou anointest my head with oil, my cup runneth over.
Surely goodness and mercy shall follow me all the days of my life:
And I will dwell in the house of the Lord for ever.

Psalm 23

Staff: *long stick used as support when walking. Also a shepherd's crook.*
Anointest my head with oil: *put a little oil on my head as a sign of a blessing.*

Psalm 23

The God of love my Shepherd is,
   And he that doth me feed;
While he is mine, and I am his,
   What can I want or need?

He leads me to the tender grass,
   Where I both feed and rest;
Then to the streams that gently pass;
   In both I have the best.

Or if I stray, he doth convert
   And bring my mind in frame;
And all this not for my desert,
   But for his holy name.

Yea, in death's shady black abode
   Well may I walk, not fear;
For thou art with me, and thy rod
   To guide, thy staff to bear.

Surely thy sweet and wondrous love
   Shall measure all my days;
And as it never shall remove,
   So neither shall my praise.

George Herbert

Convert: *put right.* **In frame:** *on the right track.* **For my desert:** *according to what I deserve.* **Abode:** *dwelling place.*

God is Our Refuge

   God is our refuge and strength, a very present help in trouble.
   Therefore will not we fear, though the earth be removed, and though the mountains be carried into the midst of the sea;
   Though the waters thereof roar and be troubled, though the mountains shake with the swelling thereof…

from Psalm 46

Refuge: *shelter.*

55

Passing Time

Elizabeth Akers Allen makes a wish many grown-ups make. But it's
impossible: we can't travel back in time. So Thomas Hood's poem about
his childhood is a wise reminder to enjoy being young while we can!
Robert Herrick and Henry Twells both warn us to make the best of the
present. Emily Brontë's poem is a conversation between an older person
and a child about the past, present and future.

from Rock Me to Sleep

Backward, turn backward, O Time, in your flight,
Make me a child again just for tonight!...

Elizabeth Akers Allen

Past and Present

I remember, I remember
The house where I was born,
The little window where the sun
Came peeping in at morn;
He never came a wink too soon
Nor brought too long a day;
But now, I often wish the night
Had borne my breath away.

I remember, I remember
The roses, red and white,
The violets, and the lily-cups,
Those flowers made of light!
The lilacs where the robin built,
And where my brother set
The laburnum on his birthday –
The tree is living yet.

I remember, I remember
Where I was used to swing,
And thought the air must rush as fresh
To swallows on the wing;
My spirit flew in feathers then
That is so heavy now,
And summer pools could hardly cool
The fever on my brow,

I remember, I remember
The fir trees dark and high;
I used to think their slender tops
Were close against the sky:
It was a childish ignorance,
But now 'tis little joy
To know I'm farther off from Heaven
Than when I was a boy.

Thomas Hood

56

The Present Time Best Pleaseth

Praise they that will times past. I joy to see
Myself now live. This age best pleaseth me.

Robert Herrick

Lines on a Clock in Chester Cathedral

When as a child, I laughed and wept,
Time crept.
When as a youth, I dreamt and talked,
Time walked.
When I became a full-grown man,
Time ran.
When older still I daily grew,
Time flew.
Soon I shall find on travelling on –
Time gone.
O Christ, wilt Thou have saved me then?
Amen.

Henry Twells

Long Life

The longer thread of life we spin,
The more occasion still to sin.

Robert Herrick

Past: Present: Future

'Tell me, tell me, smiling child,
What the past is like to thee.'
'An Autumn evening soft and mild
With a wind that sighs mournfully.'

'Tell me what is the present hour.'
'A green and flowery spray,
Where a young bird sits gathering its power
To mount and fly away.'

'And what is the future, happy one?'
'A sea beneath a cloudless sun:
A mighty glorious dazzling sea
Stretching into infinity.'

Emily Brontë

Difficult Days

It is easy to give thanks to God when things are going well. It is not so easy to be content in times of difficulty. Yet Milton managed to be content even when he lost his sight and went blind. Emily Brontë refuses ever to be afraid or cowardly, believing that whatever may happen (even should the world and the universe come to an end) God will 'never be destroyed'.

On His Blindness

When I consider how my light is spent,
   Ere half my days, in this dark world and wide,
   And that one talent which is death to hide,
Lodged with me useless, though my soul more bent
To serve therewith my Maker, and present
   My true account, lest He returning chide,
   'Doth God exact day-labour, light denied?'
I fondly ask. But patience, to prevent
That murmur, soon replies 'God doth not need
   Either man's work, or his own gifts: who best
   Bear his mild yoke, they serve him best. His state
Is kingly: thousands at his bidding speed,
   And post o'er land and ocean without rest;
   They also serve who only stand and wait.'

John Milton

My light: my ability to see. **Talent:** *Milton's ability as a writer.* **Chide:** *scold.*
Exact day-labour, light denied: *expect us to work without daylight.* **Fondly:**
foolishly. **Yoke:** *hardship.*

No Coward Soul is Mine

No coward soul is mine
No trembler in the world's storm-troubled sphere
I see Heaven's glories shine
And Faith shines equal arming me from Fear.

O God within my breast
Almighty ever-present Deity
Life, that in me hast rest
As I, Undying Life, have power in Thee.

Vain are the thousand creeds
That move men's hearts, unutterably vain,
Worthless as withered weeds
Or idlest froth amid the boundless main

To waken doubt in one
Holding so fast by thy infinity,
So surely anchored on
The steadfast rock of immortality.

With wide-embracing love
Thy spirit animates eternal years,
Pervades and broods above,
Changes, sustains, dissolves, creates and rears.

Though Earth and moon were gone,
And suns and universes ceased to be
And thou wert left alone
Every existence would exist in thee.

There is not room for Death
Nor atom that his might could render void
Since thou art Being and Breath
And what thou art may never be destroyed.

Emily Brontë

Deity: God. **Undying Life:** *God.* **Boundless main:** *the oceans.*
Immortality: *everlasting life.* **Pervades:** *penetrates.* **Void:** *ineffective, powerless.*

Happy Old Age

Lewis Carroll's well-known poem 'Father William' is a parody or joke version of a serious poem by Robert Southey. In Southey's poem, a young man asks an old man what is the best way to live your life, and gets good advice. Robert Browning assures us there is nothing to fear about getting old – if only we have faith. A similar faith is expressed in the spiritual 'Swing Low, Sweet Chariot'. It is based on the Bible story about Elijah happily going to heaven – or going home at the end of his life on Earth.

Father William

'You are old, Father William,' the young man
   cried,
  'The few locks that are left you are grey;
You are hale, Father William, a hearty old man;
   Now tell me the reason, I pray.'

'In the days of my youth,' Father William
   replied,
  'I remembered that youth would fly fast;
And abused not my health and my vigour at
   first
   That I never might need them at last.'

'You are old, Father William,' the young man
   cried,
  'And pleasures with youth pass away;
And yet you lament not the days that are gone;
   Now tell me the reason, I pray.'

'In the days of my youth,' Father William
   replied,
  'I remembered that youth could not last;
I thought of the future, whatever I did,
   That I never might grieve for the past.'

'You are old, Father William,' the young man
   cried,
  'And life must be hastening away;
You are cheerful, and love to converse upon
   death;
   Now tell me the reason, I pray.'

'I am cheerful, young man,' Father William
   replied;
  'Let the cause thy attention engage;
In the days of my youth I remembered my God,
   And He hath not forgotten my age!'

Robert Southey

Need them at last: *lack them in old age.* ***Lament:*** *regret.*

60

from You are Old, Father William

'You are old, Father William,' the young man said,
  'And your hair has become very white;
And yet you incessantly stand on your head –
  Do you think, at your age, it is right?'

'In my youth,' Father William replied to his son,
  'I feared it might injure the brain;
But now that I'm perfectly sure I have none,
  Why, I do it again and again.'…

Lewis Carroll

Incessantly: without stopping.

from Rabbi Ben Ezra

  Grow old along with me!
  The best is yet to be,
The last of life, for which the first was made:
  Our times are in His hand
  Who saith 'A whole I planned,
Youth shows but half; trust God: see all nor
  be afraid!'…

Robert Browning

Swing Low, Sweet Chariot

Swing low, sweet chariot,
Coming for to carry me home.
Swing low, sweet chariot,
Coming for to carry me home.

I looked over Jordan,
What did I see,
Coming for to carry me home?
A band of angels coming after me,
Coming for to carry me home.

I'm sometimes up and sometimes down,
Coming for to carry me home,
But still my soul feels heavenly bound,
Coming for to carry me home,

Swing low, sweet chariot,
Coming for to carry me home.
Swing low, sweet chariot,
Coming for to carry me home.

Author unknown

When Wordly Tasks Are Done

Old Father Time is usually pictured with a scythe, cutting down or 'reaping' what lies in his path. William Ernest Henley writes about him being a reaper (who 'harvests' our lives) but also as being a sower who scatters the seeds of new life. William Shakespeare and Sir Walter Raleigh, too, see the good things about dying! Shakespeare says it will be a time when we have no more work, no more fears and no more worries. Raleigh promises us that 'Time' may seem to rob us of our life – but the grave is not in fact an ending but the start of a new life.

I am the Reaper

I am the Reaper.
All things with heedful hook
Silent I gather.
Pale roses touched with the spring,
Tall corn in summer,
Fruits rich with autumn, and frail winter
　　blossoms –
Reaping, still reaping –
All things with heedful hook
Timely I gather.

I am the Sower.
All the unbodied life
Runs through my seed-sheet.
Atom with atom wed,
Each quickening the other,
Fall through my hands, ever changing, still
　　changeless.
Ceaselessly sowing,
Life, incorruptible life,
Flows from my seed-sheet.

Maker and breaker,
I am the ebb and the flood,
Here and hereafter.
Speed through the tangle and coil
Of infinite nature,
Viewless and soundless I fashion all being,
Taker and giver,
I am the womb and the grave,
The Now and the Ever.

William Ernest Henley

Seed-sheet: *perforated sheet through which seed is scattered.*
Incorruptible: *everlasting.* **Ebb and flood:** *coming and going (like the tide).*

Fear No More

Fear no more the heat o' the sun,
 Nor the furious winter's rages;
Thou thy worldly task hast done,
 Home art gone, and ta'en thy wages;
Golden lads and girls all must,
As chimney-sweepers, come to dust.

Fear no more the frown o' the great,
 Thou art past the tyrant's stroke;
Care no more to clothe and eat;
 To thee the reed is as the oak:
The sceptre, learning, physic, must
All follow this, and come to dust.

Fear no more the lightning-flash,
 Nor the all-dreaded thunder-stone;
Fear not slander, censure rash;
 Thou hast finished joy and moan:
All lovers young, all lovers must
Consign to thee, and come to dust.

No exorciser harm thee!
 Nor no witchcraft charm thee!
Ghost unlaid forbear thee!
 Nothing ill come near thee!
Quiet consummation have;
And renowned be thy grave!

William Shakespeare

*Thy worldly task: your life's work. The frown o' the
great: the anger of powerful people. Sceptre: rod (a sign of
power and authority). Physic: medicine. Censure: being
told off. Exorciser: person who raises spirits.
Consummation: completion (of life).*

His Epitaph

Even such is Time, which takes in trust
Our youth, our joys, and all we have,
And pays us but with age and dust,
Who, in the dark and silent grave,
When we have wandered all our ways,
Shuts up the story of our days.
 Yet from this earth, and grave, and dust,
 The Lord shall raise me up I trust.

Sir Walter Raleigh

In Memoriam

It is of course very sad when anyone dies but these poems are reminders that, when someone (like Lucy in Wordsworth's poem) does die, we need also to give thanks for the good things in their lives. Tennyson's poem 'In Memoriam' is a very long poem – nearly 3,000 lines long! Its title is Latin for 'in memory of' and Tennyson wrote it in memory of his best friend, Arthur Hallam who died when he was only 22. Of course, Christians (like John Donne) believe that death is not an ending but the beginning of a more glorious life in heaven where 'death' does not exist – which is why Christina Rossetti says we should not be sad about death.

Lucy

She dwelt among the untrodden ways
   Beside the springs of Dove,
A maid whom there were none to praise,
   And very few to love:

A violet by a mossy stone
   Half-hidden from the eye!
Fair as a star when only one
   Is shining in the sky.

She lived unknown, and few could know
   When Lucy ceased to be;
But she is in her grave, and, oh!
   The difference to me!

William Wordsworth

Dove: an English river. **A violet... :** *Lucy was like a hidden flower and only noticed by a few people.*

from 'In Memoriam'

Our little systems have their day:
   They have their day and cease to be:
   They are but broken lights of thee
And thou, O Lord, art more than they.

We have but faith: we cannot know;
   For knowledge is of things we see;
   And yet we trust it comes from thee,
A beam in darkness let it grow…

Be near me when my light is low,
   When the blood creeps, and the nerves prick
   And tingle; and the heart is sick,
And all the wheels of Being slow…

Be near me when I fade away,
   To point the term of human strife,
   And on the low dark verge of life
The twilight of eternal day…

Whereof the man, that with me trod
   This planet, was a noble type
   Appearing ere the times were ripe,
That friend of mine who lives in God,

That God, which ever lives and loves,
   One God, one law, one element,
   And one far-off divine event,
To which the whole creation moves.

Alfred Lord Tennyson

Little systems: our bodies. Broken lights: pale imitations.
My light: my soul. The man, that with me… : Tennyson's friend.
Ere: before. Ripe: ready.

from Death be not Proud

… One short sleep past, we wake eternally,
And Death shall be no more; Death, thou
   shalt die.

John Donne

One short sleep: dying. Eternally: for ever.

Song

When I am dead, my dearest,
   Sing no sad songs for me;
Plant thou no roses at my head,
   Nor shady cypress tree:
Be the green grass above me
   With showers and dewdrops wet;
And if thou wilt, remember,
   And if thou wilt, forget.

I shall not see the shadows,
   I shall not feel the rain;
I shall not hear the nightingale
   Sing on as if in pain:
And dreaming through the twilight
   That doth not rise nor set,
Haply I may remember,
   And haply may forget.

Christina Rossetti

Haply: perhaps.

Love Everlasting

Christians believe that, however difficult things seem to get, God is with them and ready to help if only they pray to him. As Isaac Watts says in his hymn (which is also a prayer), just as he has helped us in the past, so he will 'for years to come'. God existed before the world was created: he is also 'everlasting'. William Cullen Bryant's poem (based on a French poem) also says that, come what may, God's love for us will remain unchanged.

O God, Our Help in Ages Past

O God, our help in ages past,
   Our hope for years to come,
Our shelter from the stormy blast,
   And our eternal home.

Beneath the shadow of Thy throne
   Thy saints have dwelt secure;
Sufficient is Thine arm alone,
   And our defence is sure.

Before the hills in order stood,
   Or earth received her frame,
From everlasting Thou are God,
   To endless years the same.

A thousand ages in Thy sight
   Are like an evening gone:
Short as the watch that ends the night
   Before the rising sun.

Time, like an ever-rolling stream,
   Bears all its sons away;
They fly forgotten, as a dream
   Dies at the opening day.

O God, our help in ages past,
   Our hope for years to come,
Be Thou our guard while troubles last
   And our eternal home.

Isaac Watts

*Frame: shape. **The watch that ends the night:** a period sailors are on duty on board ship.*

The Love of God

All things that are on earth shall wholly pass away
Except the love of God, which shall live and last for aye.
The forms of men shall be as they had never been;
The blasted groves shall lose their fresh and tender green;
The birds of the thicket shall end their pleasant song,
And the nightingale shall cease to chant the evening long;
The kine of the pasture shall feel the dart that kills,
And all the fair white flocks shall perish from the hills.
The goat and antlered stag, the wolf and the fox,
The wild boar of the wood, and the chamois of the rocks,
And the strong and fearless bear, in the trodden dust shall lie;
And the dolphin of the sea and the mighty whale shall die.
And realms shall be dissolved, and empires be no more,
And they shall bow to death who ruled from shore to shore;
And the great globe itself, so the holy writings tell,
With the rolling firmament, where the starry armies dwell,
Shall melt with fervent heat – they shall all pass away
Except the love of God, which shall live and last for aye.

William Cullen Bryant
from Bernard Rascas

Aye: *ever.* **Groves:** *small woods.* **Kine:** *cattle.* **Dart:** *arrow or shot.* **Chamois:** *goat.*
Firmament: *heaven, skies.*

Life to Come?

Two of the great questions that have been asked over the ages are why there are so many troubles in this life and what will be our reward (if any) at the end of this life. Christina Rossetti asks both questions in her poem 'Uphill'. Is life an 'uphill' struggle 'to the very end'? And what lies at the end of life's journey? Emily Dickinson also wonders what lies at the end of this life: will there be a new life (or, as she puts it) a new morning? In George Herbert's poem, a heavenly echo provides some of the answers to his questions.

Uphill

'Does the road wind uphill all the way?'
   'Yes, to the very end.'
'Will the day's journey take the whole long day?'
   'From morn to night, my friend.'

'But is there for the night a resting-place?'
   'A roof for when the slow, dark hours begin.'
'May not the darkness hide it from my face?'
   'You cannot miss that inn.'

'Shall I meet other wayfarers at night?'
   'Those who have gone before.'
'Then must I knock, or call when just in sight?'
   'They will not keep you standing at that door.'

'Shall I find comfort, travel-sore and weak?'
   'Of labour you shall find the sum.'
'Will there be beds for me and all who seek?'
   'Yea, beds for all who come.'

Christina Rossetti

Will There Really
be a Morning?

Will there really be a morning?
Is there such a thing as day?
Could I see it from the mountains
If I were as tall as they?

Emily Dickinson

Heaven

O, who will show me those delights on high?
   Echo: *I.*
Thou Echo, thou art mortal, all men know.
   Echo: *No.*
Wert thou not born among the trees and leaves?
   Echo: *Leaves.*
And are there any leaves that still abide?
   Echo: *Bide.*
What leaves are they? Impart the matter wholly.
   Echo: *Holy.*
Are holy leaves the Echo, then, of bliss?
   Echo: *Yes.*
Then tell me, what is that supreme delight?
   Echo: *Light.*
Light to the mind; what shall the will enjoy?
   Echo: *Joy.*
But are there cares and business with the pleasure?
   Echo: *Leisure.*
Light, joy, and leisure; but shall they persever?
   Echo: *Ever.*

George Herbert

Abide: *remain.* **Persever:** *last for ever.*

Life to Come!

Christians believe they will reach paradise or heaven at the end of their lives. Robert Herrick is sure that, for this reason, there is no need to be afraid of dying. Henry Vaughan is equally certain that, with the help of Jesus (his 'gracious Friend'), 'the good' shall find the peace of new life in heaven, while Bishop William Walsham How believes that, although life on earth may at times be a battle, God is with us and wil help us reach 'the calm of Paradise'.

His Creed

I do believe, that die I must
And be returned from out my dust:
I do believe that, when I rise,
Christ I shall see with these same eyes:
I do believe that I must come,
With others, to the dreadful doom:
I do believe the bad must go
From thence, to everlasting woe.
I do believe the good and I
Shall live with Him eternally:
I do believe I shall inherit
Heaven by Christ's mercies – not my merit:
I do believe the One in Three
And Three in perfect unity:
Lastly that Jesus is a deed
Of gift from God: And here's my Creed.

Robert Herrick

Everlasting woe: separation from Jesus; hell. **Inherit:** *receive, be allowed to enter.* **Deed of gift:** *a promised gift.*

Peace

My soul, there is a country
　Afar beyond the stars,
Where stands a winged sentry,
　All skilful in the wars.
There, above noise and danger,
　Sweet peace sits crowned with smiles,
And One born in a manger
　Commands the beauteous files.
He is thy gracious Friend,
　And (O my soul awake!)
Did in pure love descend
　To die here for thy sake.
If thou canst get but thither,
　There grows the flower of peace –
The rose that cannot wither –
　Thy fortress, and thy ease.
Leave, then, thy foolish ranges,
　For none can thee secure
But One who never changes –
　Thy God, thy Life, thy Cure.

Henry Vaughan

Ranges: where you live.

70

For All the Saints

For all the saints who from their labours rest,
Who thee by faith before the world confessed,
Thy name, O Jesu, be for ever blest.
   Alleluia!

Thou wast their rock, their fortress, and their might;
Thou, Lord, their Captain in the well-fought fight;
Thou, in the darkness, still their one true light.
   Alleluia!

O may thy soldiers, faithful, true, and bold,
Fight as the saints who nobly fought of old,
And win, with them, the victor's crown of gold.
   Alleluia!

O blest communion, fellowship divine!
We feebly struggle, they in glory shine;
Yet all are one in thee, for all are thine.
   Alleluia!

And when the strife is fierce, the warfare long,
Steals on the ear the distant triumph-song,
And hearts are brave again and arms are strong.
   Alleluia!

The golden evening brightens in the west;
Soon, soon to faithful warriors comes their rest:
Sweet is the calm of Paradise the blest.
   Alleluia!

But lo, there breaks a yet more glorious day;
The saints triumphant rise in bright array:
The King of Glory passes on his way.
   Alleluia!

From earth's wide bounds, from ocean's
   farthest coast,
Through gates of pearl streams in the
   countless host,
Singing to Father, Son and Holy Ghost
Alleluia!

Bishop William Walsham How

*Confessed: said firmly, announced. **Alleluia**: 'God be praised'. **Fight**: the struggle to live life. **Soldiers**: all Christians. **Communion**: band or company of friends, other Christians. **Strife, warfare**: life's 'battle'. **Steals on the ear**: begins to be heard. **Golden evening**: sunset; the later years of life. **King of Glory**: Jesus. **Gates of pearl**: entrance to heaven. **Countless host**: all those entering heaven.*

Born This Happy Morning

Over the years, poets have told many stories about the great festival of Christmas which celebrates the birth of Jesus in Bethlehem. Two unknown poets make us think what it was like in the stable where Jesus was born – and both describe the peace and stillness of that scene. For a much later poet, Robert Herrick, the birth of Jesus is so wonderful it makes the whole earth smile.

The Chester Carol

He who made the earth so fair
Slumbers in a stable bare,
Warmed by cattle standing there.

Oxen, lowing, stand all round;
In the stall no other sound
Mars the peace by Mary found.

Joseph piles the soft, sweet hay,
Starlight drives the dark away,
Angels sing a heavenly lay.

Jesu sleeps in Mary's arm;
Sheltered there from rude alarm,
None can do Him ill or harm.

See His mother o'er Him bend;
Hers the joy to soothe and tend,
Hers the bliss that knows no end.

Author unknown

*Lay: song. **Rude:** rough, sudden.*

Christmas Morning

Why does the chilling winter's morn
Smile like a field beset with corn?
Or smell like to a mead new shorn,
Thus, on the sudden?

Come and see
The cause why things thus fragrant be.
'Tis He is born whose quickening birth
Gives life and lustre, public mirth,
To heaven and the under-earth.

We see Him come and know Him ours
Who, with His sunshine and His showers,
Turns all the patient ground to flowers.

The darling of the world is come,
And fit it is we find a room
To welcome Him.

Robert Herrick

Beset with: *full of.* **Mead:** *meadow, field.*
Quickening: *life-bringing.* **Lustre:** *joyful glow.*

Mother and Maiden
(also known as
'As Dew in April')

I sing of a maiden
　　That is matchless;
King of all kings
　　To her son she chose.

He came all so still
　　Where his mother was,
As dew in April
　　That falleth on the grass.

He came all so still
　　To his mother's bower,
As dew in April
　　That falleth on the flower.

He came all so still –
　　There his mother lay,
As dew in April
　　That falleth on the spray.

Mother and maiden
　　Was never none but she;
Well may such a lady
　　God's mother be.

Author unknown

The Three Kings

In the Bible, it says that certain 'wise men' or 'kings' from the East came to Jerusalem, having seen a bright star in the sky. They believed this star was a sign that a great king had been born. It led them to Bethlehem where they found the baby Jesus and gave him presents of gold and frankincense and myrrh. Longfellow's poem retells the story, adding details linked with the story (such as the names of the wise men) but which are not actually in the Bible. The king of the country where Jesus was born was a jealous man called Herod.

The Three Kings

Three kings came riding from far away,
   Melchior and Gaspar and Baltasar;
Three Wise Men out of the East were they,
And they travelled by night and they slept by day,
   For their guide was a beautiful, wonderful star.

The star was so beautiful, large and clear
   That all the other stars of the sky
Became a white mist in the atmosphere;
And by this they knew that the coming was near
   Of the Prince foretold in the prophecy.

Three caskets they bore on their saddlebows,
   Three caskets of gold with golden keys;
Their robes were of crimson silk with rows
Of bells and pomegranates and furbelows,
   Their turbans like blossoming almond trees.

And so the Three Kings rode into the West,
   Through the dusk of night over hill and dell,
And sometimes they nodded with beard on breast,
And sometimes talked, as they paused to rest,
   With the people they met at some wayside well.

Of the Child that is born, said Baltasar,
   'Good people, I pray you, tell us the news;
For we in the East have seen His star,
And have ridden fast, and have ridden far,
   To find and worship the King of the Jews.'

And the people answered: 'You ask in vain;
   We know of no King but Herod the Great!'
They thought the Wise Men were men insane
As they spurred their horses across the plain,
   Like riders in haste, and who cannot wait.

And when they came to Jerusalem,
   Herod the Great, who had heard this thing,
Sent for the Wise Men and questioned them;
And said: 'Go down unto Bethlehem,
   And bring me tidings of this new King.'

So they rode away; and the star stood still,
   The only one in the grey of morn;
Yes, it stopped, it stood still of its own free will,
Right over Bethlehem on the hill,
   The city of David, where Christ was born.

And the Three Kings rode through the gate and
   the guard,
   Through the silent street, till their horses
     turned
And neighed as they entered the great inn-yard;
But the windows were closed and the doors
   were barred,
   And only a light in the stable burned.

And cradled there in the scented hay,
   In the air made sweet by the breath of kine,
The little Child in the manger lay,
The Child that would be King one day
   Of a kingdom not human but divine.

His mother, Mary of Nazareth,
   Sat watching beside His place of rest,
Watching the even flow of His breath,
For the joy of life and the terror of death
   Were mingled together in her breast.

They laid their offerings at His feet;
   The gold was their tribute to a King,
The frankincense, with its odour sweet,
Was for the Priest, the Paraclete,
   The myrrh for the body's burying.

And the mother wondered and bowed her head,
   And sat as still as a statue of stone;
Her heart was troubled yet comforted,
Remembering what the angel had said
   Of the endless reign and of David's throne.

Then the Kings rode out of the city gate,
   With a clatter of hoofs in proud array;
But they went not back to Herod the Great,
For they knew his malice and feared his hate,
   And returned to their homes by another way.

Henry Wadsworth Longfellow

Saddlebow: *the front of a saddle.* **Furbelows:** *decorative trimmings.*
Kine: *cattle.* **Paraclete:** *the Holy Spirit.*

Celebrating Christmas

Many Christmas carols repeat the wish that there will be 'peace on earth, good will to men'. These Christmas poems and songs also remind us of the customs (such as carol singing) associated with Christmas. Longfellow points out that, even if a war is being fought at Christmas time (so that it seems as if good things are being defeated by evil), God will triumph in the end, bringing peace on Earth.

Wassail Song

Here we come a-wassailing
  Among the leaves so green,
Here we come a-wandering,
  So fair to be seen.
  Love and joy come to you,
  And to you your wassail too,
  And God bless you, and send you
  A happy new year.

We are not daily beggars
  That beg from door to door,
But we are neighbours' children
  Whom you have seen before.

God bless the master of this house,
  Likewise the mistress too;
And all the children
  That round the table go;

And all your kin and kinsfolk,
  That dwell both far and near;
We wish you a Merry Christmas,
  And a Happy New Year.

Old English song

Wassail: *to drink someone's good health.*
Kin and kinsfolk: *relatives.*

Deck the Hall with Holly

Deck the hall with boughs of holly,
Fa la la la la la la la la,
'Tis the season to be jolly,
Fa la la la la la la la la,
Fill the mead cup, raise the wassail,
Fa la la fa la la la la la,
Sing the ancient Christmas carol,
Fa la la la la la la la la,

See the flowing bowl before us,
Strike the harp and join the chorus,
Follow me in merry measure,
While I sing of mirth and pleasure.

Fast away the Old Year passes,
Hail the New, ye lads and lasses,
Singing gaily all together
Heedless of the wind and weather.

A Welsh carol for the New Year

Christmas Bells

I heard the bells on Christmas Day
Their old familiar carols play,
 And wild and sweet
 The words repeat
Of Peace on earth, Good-will to men!

And thought how, as the day had come,
The belfries of all Christendom
 Had rolled along
 The unbroken song
Of Peace on earth, Good-will to men!

Till ringing, singing on its way,
The world revolved from night to day,
 A voice, a chime,
 A chant sublime,
Of Peace on earth, Good-will to men!

Then from each black accursed mouth,
The cannon thundered in the South,
 And with the sound
 The carols drowned,
The Peace on earth, Good-will to men!

And in despair I bowed my head;
'There is no peace on earth,' I said,
 'For hate is strong
 And mocks the song
Of Peace on earth, Good-will to men!'

Then peeled the bells more loud and deep;
'God is not dead, nor doth he sleep!
 The Wrong shall fail,
 The Right prevail,
With Peace on earth, Good-will to men!'

Henry Wadsworth Longfellow

Now Thrice Welcome Christmas

Now thrice welcome, Christmas,
 Which brings us good cheer,
Minc'd pies and plum porridge,
 Good ale and strong beer;
With pig, goose and capon,
 The best that can be,
So well doth the weather
 And our stomachs agree.

With holly and ivy
 So green and so gay,
We deck up our houses
 As fresh as the day,
With bays and rosemary,
 And laurel complete;
And every one now
Is a king in conceit.

Author unknown

*Capon: chicken. **Bays**: leaves of an evergreen tree.*
In conceit: in one's imagination.

A Bunch of Holly

But give me holly, bold and jolly,
Honest, prickly, shining holly;
Pluck me holly leaf and berry
For the day when I make merry.

Christina Rossetti

Jesus

'God is love.' That is a very simple statement, but what does it mean?
George Herbert suggests love is so wonderful that we are sometimes afraid of
it while John Clare seems to be saying that love is simply a glorious mystery.
For the unknown author of 'The Holy Well', God's love is made real in the
person of Jesus – even when he was still a young boy.

Love

Love bade me welcome; yet my soul drew back,
  Guilty of dust and sin,
But quick-eyed Love, observing me grow slack
  From my first entrance in,
Drew nearer to me, sweetly questioning,
  If I lacked anything.

'A guest', I answered, 'worthy to be here.'
  Love said, 'You shall be he.'
'I, the unkind, ungrateful? Ah, my dear,
  I cannot look on thee.'
Love took my hand, and smiling did reply,
  'Who made the eyes but I?'

'Truth, Lord, but I have marred them; let my shame
  Go where it doth deserve.'
'And know you not', says Love, 'who bore the blame?'
  'My dear, then I will serve.'
'You must sit down', says Love, 'and taste my meat.'
  So I did sit and eat.

George Herbert

Marred: spoiled.

Love Lives Beyond

Love lives beyond
The tomb – the earth – which fades like dew.
I love the fond,
The faithful and the true.

Love lives in sleep;
The happiness of healthy dreams
Eve's dews may weep
But love delightful seems.

'Tis seen in flowers
And in the even's pearly dew.
On earth's green hours
And in the heaven's eternal blue.

'Tis heard in Spring
When light and sunbeams warm and kind
On angel's wing
Bring love and music to the mind;

And where is voice
So young and beautifully sweet
As nature's choice
When Spring and lovers meet?

Love lives beyond
The tomb, the earth, the flowers and dew;
I love the fond,
The faithful, young and true.

John Clare

The even's: the evening's.

The Holy Well

As it fell out one May morning,
 And upon a bright holiday,
Sweet Jesus asked of his dear mother
 If he might go to play.
'To play, to play, sweet Jesus shall go,
 And to play now get you gone;
And let me hear of no complaint
 At night when you come home.'

Sweet Jesus went down to yonder town,
 As far as the Holy Well,
And there did see as fine children
 As any tongue can tell.
He said, 'God bless you every one,
 And your bodies Christ save and see!
And now, little children, I'll play with you,
 And you shall play with me.'

But they made answer to him, 'No!
 Thou art meaner than us all;
Thou art but a simple fair maid's child,
 Born in an ox's stall.'
Sweet Jesus turned him round about,
 Neither laughed, nor smiled, nor spoke;
But the tears came trickling from his eyes
 Like waters from the rock.

Sweet Jesus turned him round about,
 To his mother's dear home went he,
And said, 'I have been in yonder town,
 As after you may see:
I have been down in yonder town,
 As far as the Holy Well;
There did I meet with as fine children
 As any tongue can tell.

'I said, "God bless you every one,
 And your bodies Christ save and see!
And now, little children, I'll play with you,
 And you shall play with me."
But they made answer to me "No";
 They were lords' and ladies' sons,
And I the meanest of them all,
 Born in an ox's stall.'

'Though you are but a maiden's child,
 Born in an ox's stall,
Thou art the Christ, the King of Heaven,
 And the Saviour of them all!
Sweet Jesus, go down to yonder town,
 As far as the Holy Well,
And take away those sinful souls,
 And dip them deep in hell.'

'Nay, nay,' sweet Jesus smiled and said;
 'Nay, nay, that may not be,
For there are too many sinful souls
 Crying out for the help of me.'
Then up spoke the angel Gabriel,
 Upon a good set steven,
'Although you are but a maiden's child,
 You are the King of Heaven!'

Author unknown (sixteenth century)

Yonder: distant. **Meanest:** lowliest. **Steven:** loud voice.

Good Friday

For Christians, Good Friday is a sad day. It's when they remember how Jesus gave himself up to be put to death by crucifixion just outside the city of Jerusalem, as Cecil Frances Alexander describes in her famous hymn. And his execution was painful and sad – and he was buried in a grave as Robert Herrick reminds us. But, as we shall see, Friday was not the end of the story – which is why it is known as Good Friday.

There is a Green Hill

There is a green hill far away,
  Without a city wall,
Where the dear Lord was crucified,
  Who died to save us all.

We may not know, we cannot tell,
  What pains He had to bear,
But we believe it was for us
  He hung and suffered there.

He died that we might be forgiven,
  He died to make us good,
That we might go at last to heaven,
  Saved by His precious blood.

There was no other good enough
  To pay the price of sin;
He only could unlock the gate
  Of heaven, and let us in.

Oh, dearly, dearly has he loved,
  And we must love Him too,
And trust in His redeeming blood,
  And try His works to do.

Cecil Frances Alexander

Without a city wall: outside a city wall.

from Christ Going to His Cross

Put off thy robe of purple, then go on
To the sad place of execution:
Thine hour is come, and the tormentor stands
Ready to pierce thy tender feet and hands.
Long before this the base, the dull, the rude,
The inconstant and unpurged multitude
Yawn for thy coming. Some ere this time cry:
'How he defers! How loath he is to die!'
Amongst this scum the soldier with his spear,
And that sour fellow with his vinegar,
His sponge, and stick, do ask why thou dost stay…

Not as a thief shalt thou ascend the mount,
But like a person of some high account:
The cross shall be thy stage, and thou shalt there
The spacious field have for thy theatre…

Robert Herrick

Before this: *in front of this.* **Inconstant:** *changing their minds.*
Unpurged: *not saved.* **Defers:** *lingers.*

He is Risen

Jesus was crucified on Good Friday. Three days later, on the first Easter Sunday, Christians believe he rose from the dead and came back to life. The unknown author of 'All in the Morning' remembers various important events in the life of Jesus from his birth to the week leading up to his crucifixion – and then, most importantly of all, his rising from the dead. Edmund Spenser explains the importance of that event. By his suffering, Jesus has saved each one of us. Christians believe that, like William Cowper's wounded deer, we are all in need of being rescued, healed and given new life, through Jesus Christ.

All in the Morning

It was on Christmas Day
  And all in the morning,
Our Saviour was born
And our heavenly King:
  And was not this a joyful thing!
  And sweet Jesus they called him by name…

It was on the Twelfth Day,
  And all in the morning,
The Wise Men were led
To our heavenly King:
  And was not this a joyful thing?
  And sweet Jesus they called him by name…

It was on Holy Wednesday,
  And all in the morning,
That Judas betrayed
Our dear heavenly King:
  And was not this a woeful thing?
  And sweet Jesus we'll call him by name.

It was on Sheer Thursday,
  And all in the morning,
They plaited a crown of thorns
For our heavenly King:
  And was not this a woeful thing?
  And sweet Jesus we'll call him by name.

It was on Good Friday,
  And all in the morning,
They crucified our Saviour,
And our heavenly King:
  And was not this a woeful thing?
  And sweet Jesus we'll call him by name.

It was on Easter Day,
  And all in the morning,
Our Saviour arose,
  Our own heavenly King:
  The sun and the moon they did both rise
    with him,
  And sweet Jesus we'll call him by name.

Author unknown

Sheer Thursday: Maundy Thursday, the day before Good Friday ('sheer' is an old word meaning 'clean' or 'pure').

Easter Sunday

Most glorious Lord of life! That, on this day,
Didst make Thy triumph over death and sin:
And, having harrowed hell, didst bring away
Captivity thence captive, us to win:
This joyous day, dear Lord, with joy begin,
And grant that we, for whom thou diddest die,
Being with Thy dear blood clean washed from sin,
May live for ever in felicity!
And that Thy love we weighing worthily,
May likewise love Thee for the same again;
And for Thy sake, that all like dear didst buy,
With love may one another entertain!
    So let us love, dear Love, like as we ought,
    – Love is the lesson which the Lord us taught.

Edmund Spenser

Triumph over death: coming back to life. **Harrowed hell:** *rescued those in hell.* **Felicity:** *happiness.*

The Stricken Deer
(from The Task)

I was a stricken deer, that left the herd
Long since: with many an arrow deep infixed
My panting side was charged, when I withdrew
To seek a tranquil death in distant shades.
There was I found by One who had Himself
Been hurt by the archers. In His side He bore,
And in His hands and feet, the cruel scars.
With gentle force soliciting the darts,
He drew them forth, and healed, and bade me live...

William Cowper

Stricken: wounded, distressed. **Shades:** *shadowy, private places.* **One who had Himself been hurt:** *Jesus who had been crucified.* **Soliciting:** *removing.* **Bade:** *told.*

Ready for the Lord

Suppose a king said he was coming to visit us – we would make our house look as fine as possible. But what would we do if we heard Jesus was going to visit us? The unknown author of 'Preparations' suggests that, although he has said he will return, we are doing very little to make our lives ready for him. Meanwhile William Blake wonders if Jesus ever visited England during his first time on earth – but prays for determination and then vows to do all he can to make ready for His next coming.

Preparations

Yet if His Majesty, our sovereign lord,
Should of his own accord
Friendly himself invite,
And say, 'I'll be your guest to-morrow night,'
How should we stir ourselves, call and command
All hands to work! 'Let no man idle stand.

'Set me fine Spanish tables in the hall;
See they be fitted all;
Let there be room to eat
And order taken that there want no meat.
See every sconce and candlestick made bright,
That without tapers they may give a light.

'Look to the presence: are the carpets spread,
The dazie o'er the head,
The cushions in the chairs,
And all the candles lighted on the stairs?
Perfume the chambers, and in any case
Let each man give attendance in his place!'

Thus, if a king were coming, would we do;
And 'twere good reason too;
For 'tis a duteous thing
To show all honour to an earthly king,
And after all our travail and our cost,
So he be pleased, to think no labour lost.

But at the coming of the King of Heaven
All's set at six and seven;
We wallow in our sin,
Christ cannot find a chamber in the inn.
We entertain Him always like a stranger,
And, as at first, still lodge Him in the manger.

Author unknown

*Sconce: fire screen. **Tapers:** candles. **Dazie:** canopy. **Travail:** work.*

A New Jerusalem

And did those feet in ancient time
Walk upon England's mountains green?
And was the Holy Lamb of God
On England's pleasant pastures seen?

And did the countenance divine
Shine forth upon our clouded hills?
And was Jerusalem builded here
Among these dark satanic mills?

Bring me my bow of burning gold!
Bring me my arrows of desire!
Bring me my spear! O clouds, unfold!
Bring me my chariot of fire!

I will not cease from mental fight,
Nor shall my sword sleep in my hand,
Till we have built Jerusalem
In England's green and pleasant land.

William Blake

Dark satanic mills: *factories.*
Jerusalem: *(here) the Kingdom of God.*

The Voyage of Life

Many poets have written about life as though it is a journey or a voyage through all sorts of difficulties – until we reach a happy resting place. In 'Henry Hudson's Last Voyage', Henry van Dyke imagines Hudson describing his attempt to sail round the north of America – through what is now called Hudson's Bay. This is the last verse of that poem, in which he speaks of his trust in God. Christina Rossetti's short poem consists of four riddles and their answers. Finally, an unknown author writes about a sailor who puts to sea, confident he will survive the voyage (even if 'landsmen' or others are afraid or lack faith).

What are Heavy?
Sea-sand and Sorrow

What are heavy? Sea-sand and sorrow:
What are brief? To-day and to-morrow:
What are frail? Spring blossoms and youth:
What are deep? The ocean and truth.

Christina Rossetti

Henry Hudson's Last Voyage

… Yes, I seek it still –
My great adventure and my guiding star!
For look ye, friends, our voyage is not done;
We hold by hope as long as life endures!
Somewhere among these floating fields of ice,
Somewhere along this westward widening bay,
Somewhere beneath this luminous northern
  night,
The channel opens to the Farthest East –
I know it – and some day a little ship
Will push her bowsprit in, and battle through!
And why not ours – tomorrow – who can tell?
The lucky chance awaits the fearless heart!
These are the longest days of all the year;
The world is round and God is everywhere,
And while our shallop floats we still can steer.
So point her up, John King, nor'-west by north,
We'll keep the honour of a certain aim
Amid the peril of uncertain ways,
And sail ahead, and leave the rest to God.

Henry van Dyke

Shallop: *type of boat or ship with several masts.* **John King:** *the sailor who steered Hudson's ship.*

Jack the Guinea-pig

When the anchor's weigh'd and the ship's
   unmoored,
And the landsmen lag behind sir,
The sailor joyful skips on board,
And, swearing, prays for a wind, sir
   Towing here,
   Yehoing there,
   Steadily, readily,
   Cheerily, merrily,
Still from care and thinking free,
Is a sailor's life, at sea.

When we sail with a fresh'ning breeze,
And landsmen all grow sick, sir,
The sailor lolls, with his mind at ease,
And the song and the can go quick, sir:
   Laughing here,
   Quaffing there,
   Steadily, readily,
   Cheerily, merrily,
Still from care and thinking free,
Is a sailor's life, at sea.

When the wind at night whistles o'er the deep,
And sings to landsmen dreary,
The sailor fearless goes to sleep,
Or takes his watch most cheery:
   Boozing here,
   Snoozing there,
   Steadily, readily,
   Cheerily, merrily,
Still from care and thinking free,
Is a sailor's life, at sea.

When the sky grows black and the wind blows
   hard
And landsmen skulk below, sir,
Jack mounts up to the top sail yard,
And turns his quid as he goes, sir:
   Hauling here,
   Bawling there,
   Steadily, readily,
   Cheerily, merrily,
Still from care and thinking free,
Is a sailor's life, at sea.

When the foaming waves run mountains high,
And landsmen cry 'All's gone', sir,
The sailor hangs 'twixt sea and sky,
And he jokes with Davy Jones, sir!
   Dashing here,
   Clashing there,
   Steadily, readily,
   Cheerily, merrily,
Still from care and thinking free,
Is a sailor's life, at sea.

When the ship, d'ye see, becomes a wreck,
And landsmen hoist the boat, sir,
The sailor scorns to quit the deck,
While a single plank's afloat, sir:
   Swearing here,
   Tearing there,
   Steadily, readily,
   Cheerily, merrily,
Still from care and thinking free,
Is a sailor's life, at sea.

Author unknown

Guinea-pig: *sea slang for an ordinary sailor or midshipman.* **Weigh'd:** *raised, lifted.* **Landsmen:** *people not used to being at sea.*
Yehoing: *singing while pulling on the ropes.* **Can:** *cup (from which the sailors drink).* **Quaffing:** *drinking.* **The deep:** *the ocean.*
Below: *below decks.* **Yard:** *pole fastened to ship's mast, from which a sail hangs.* **Turns his quid:** *chews his tobacco, changes its position*
in his mouth. **Jokes with Davy Jones:** *laughs about dying.*

The Poets

John Barbour (1316?–95) was a Scottish poet and clergyman who probably studied and taught at Oxford and in Paris. He wrote his long poem in praise of the Scottish king, Robert the Bruce, about 1375.

Lady Julian of Norwich (1342?–1413) was an 'anchoress' or nun who lived alone in one room attached to St Julian's church in Norwich. During an illness, she had a number of strange visions or dreams which she wrote down in a book – the first book to be written in English by a woman.

Sir Walter Raleigh (1552?–1618) was a famous English explorer, who made several voyages of discovery to the American continent. He was a great favourite of Queen Elizabeth I but became unpopular and was eventually executed. He wrote many poems but most have been lost.

Edmund Spenser (1552?–99) was probably related to the Spencers of Althorp (Princess Diana's family) but lived mainly in Ireland. His most famous poem (a very long one) is called 'The Faerie Queene' which is about King Arthur and his knights but also praises Queen Elizabeth I.

Michael Drayton (1563–1631) wrote a great quantity of religious and other verse which was published in a number of books. Apart from the facts that he was born in Warwickshire and is buried in Westminster Abbey, we know very little about him.

William Shakespeare (1564–1616) is the greatest English playwright. He wrote 37 plays, mainly in verse – and several great poems as well. Although he spent most of his working life in London, he is especially linked with his home town of Stratford-upon-Avon.

Sir Henry Wotton (1568–1639) was the English ambassador in Venice and wrote a book on architecture as well as a collection of poems.

John Donne (1571?–1631) was a poet and a clergyman who became Dean of St Paul's Cathedral in London. Before that, he had been an explorer. His surname is pronounced 'dun'.

Ben Jonson (1572–1637) wrote several plays which made fun of people who were greedy, mean or unlikeable in other ways. Shakespeare acted in one of his plays. In 1616, Jonson was given a pension by the king and so, in effect, became the first 'Poet Laureate' or 'official' poet of England.

Robert Herrick (1591–1674) was a great admirer of Ben Jonson. After working as a goldsmith, he became a clergyman in Devon and wrote many religious poems, including a collection of short ones (including the ones in this book) called *Noble Numbers*.

George Herbert (1593–1633) was also a country clergyman and was nicknamed 'Holy Mr Herbert'. He wrote a collection of 160 religious poems, several of which have been set to music and are now sung as hymns.

John Milton (1608–74) is sometimes said to be the second greatest English poet after Shakespeare. His most famous poem (a very long one indeed) is called 'Paradise Lost' which retells the story of Adam and Eve. It was written after he went blind.

Henry Vaughan (1622–95) was a Welshman who worked as a doctor of medicine in the part of Wales known as Brecknock. Like George Herbert, he wrote a collection of religious poems.

John Bunyan (1628–88) was first a tinsmith then a soldier. In 1653, he joined a non-conformist church in Bedford and was imprisoned for preaching without permission. Refusing to keep the law (which said only men who had been licensed to preach could do so), he was kept in prison for twelve years. His most famous book is *Pilgrim's Progress*.

Jonathan Swift (1667–1745) was an Irishman who became a clergyman and is often known as Dean Swift. He wrote many poems, letters and political articles or pamphlets but is best remembered as the author of the story *Gulliver's Travels* – the only thing he wrote for which he received any payment (and that was £200).

Isaac Watts (1674–1748) is remembered chiefly as the first modern hymn writer. Earlier poets had had their poems set to music so that they could be sung: Isaac Watts wrote his specially to be sung. One of his best known ones begins: 'When I survey the wondrous cross…'

William Cowper (1731–1800) was a lawyer and also suffered from serious fits of depression. He wrote 68 hymns for a collection called *The Olney Hymns* and later wrote many fine poems – some of them funny, some sad. His surname is pronounced 'cooper'.

Lady Anne Lindsay (1750–1825) wrote a number of ballads and poems. She became Lady Anne Barnard after her marriage and travelled with her husband to South Africa. She wrote a long description of how the British took possession of Capetown.

William Blake (1757–1827) never went to school. It was only after he married that his wife Catherine taught him to read and write. Nevertheless, he became a great artist and poet. He wrote two collections of poems: *Songs of Innocence* and *Songs of Experience* both of which he illustrated himself. He hated the way new factories were being built all over England.

William Wordsworth (1770–1850) was born in and loved the English Lake District. Many of his poems describe (in quite simple language)

the world of nature that he saw around him. He believed that children were often wiser than over-educated adults. His writing became very popular and he was made Poet Laureate in 1843.

Samuel Taylor Coleridge (1772–1834) was a great friend of Wordsworth: they wrote a book of poems together called *Lyrical Ballads* which includes Coleridge's longest and most famous poem, *The Rime [Rhyme] of the Ancient Mariner*. He believed the first aim of poetry is to give pleasure.

Robert Southey (1774–1843) was expelled from school for writing an essay saying boys should not be beaten. He went to Cambridge University and became friendly with Coleridge. He wrote many poems and other books and was Poet Laureate before Wordsworth.

John Clare (1793–1864) worked as a ploughboy and gardener. A local bookseller published a collection of his beautiful poems about the countryside and it sold many copies. But Clare's health was not good and in 1837 he was certified as insane. He spent the rest of his life in an asylum.

William Cullen Bryant (1794–1878) was born in Massachusetts in the USA, worked as a lawyer and then as a journalist and for almost fifty years edited *The New York Evening Post*. He greatly opposed slavery and wrote many poems and hymns, and was regarded as the greatest American poet of his time.

John Keats (1795–1821) was born in London and started to train as a doctor but decided to be a poet. Despite the musical sound of his verse, it was not popular at first and he was laughed at as a 'cockney poet'. He developed tuberculosis (an illness of the lungs) and went to live in the warmer climate of Italy but died there aged only 25.

Thomas Hood (1799–1845) edited various magazines and wrote for others including *Punch*. He wrote a number of humorous poems as well as more serious ones but he did not make enough money from them to look after his family and had to go abroad for some years to avoid paying his debts.

Sara Coleridge (1802–52) was the daughter of Samuel Taylor Coleridge (see above). She wrote a long, romantic fairy tale about pirates, flying sea monsters and a fairy prince – as well as a number of other poems.

Henry Wadsworth Longfellow (1807–82) was born in Maine and grew up to become Professor of Modern Languages at Harvard University. His best known poem is 'The Song of Hiawatha' in which he retells several American Indian stories but he published many other collections of poems.

Alfred Lord Tennyson (1809–92) became really famous in 1850 when he published his long poem called 'In Memoriam' in which he expresses his sorrow for a friend who had died some years before. Also in 1850, Tennyson became Poet Laureate. He was a very popular poet in Victorian times.

Robert Browning (1812–89) is best remembered for his long 'story-poem' 'The Pied Piper of Hamelin' but he wrote many others, some which are difficult to understand. In 1846, he married Elizabeth Barrett (also a poet) but her father did not approve and they had to run away to Italy to be together.

Cecil Frances Alexander (1818–95) was born and lived in Ireland. She married a bishop and wrote over 400 poems and hymns, most of them being for children. Her most famous Christmas hymn begins 'Once in royal David's city…'

Emily Brontë (1818–48) is famous for her novel *Wuthering Heights* which takes place on the bleak Yorkshire moors where Emily lived with her sisters, Charlotte and Anne, who also wrote novels. Before any of them published their novels, Charlotte and Emily produced a book of their poems.

Julia Ward Howe (1819–1910) was born in New York and became a leading suffragette or fighter for women's rights. She won fame both as a writer and a speaker, but is now remembered for her 'Battle-Hymn of the Republic', written during the American Civil War to encourage the soldiers of the North fighting for the freedom of the slaves.

Walt Whitman (1819–92) was born on Long Island, New York. His best known collection of poems is called *Leaves of Grass*. When it appeared, another writer (Emerson) said it was 'the most extraordinary piece of wit and wisdom that America has yet contributed'. During the American Civil War, Whitman worked as a hospital visitor.

Bishop William Walsham How (1823–97) did much to help the poor in London's East End. He wrote or edited various books of prayers and hymns – and wrote 54 hymns himself. He was nicknamed 'the children's bishop' because he wrote hymns for young people to sing.

Henry Twells (1823–1900) was an English clergyman and schoolteacher. He wrote a number of hymns and helped to edit a new edition of the famous hymn book *Hymns Ancient and Modern*.

Emily Dickinson (1830–86) was born in Massachusetts in the USA and lived there, almost secretly and seeing very few people. Only two of her poems were published while she was alive (and that was against her wishes) but over a thousand were found after her death. It was many years later that she finally came to be regarded as a great poet.

Christina Rossetti (1830–94) wrote many religious and many children's poems. (Her grandfather had her first ones published when she was twelve.) Some are quite gloomy; others cheerful and full of hope. The family was originally Italian and her brother, Dante Gabriel Rossetti, was both a painter and a poet.

The Revd Charles Dodgson (1832–98) taught mathematics at Oxford University but called himself 'Lewis Carroll' when writing his stories for children, the most famous being *Alice in Wonderland* and *Through the Looking Glass*. These stories contain several 'nonsense' poems.

Elizabeth Akers Allen (1832–1912) wrote five books of poetry, her most famous poem being 'Rock Me to Sleep, Mother' which became a popular song during the American Civil War. She also wrote many humorous letters describing her travels in America and Europe. These were published under the name Florence Percy.

Folliott Pierpoint (1835–1917) was a schoolmaster who taught Latin and Greek. He wrote three books of poetry and a number of hymns.

Thomas Hardy (1840–1928) is famous for his novels set in the county of Dorset which he called 'Wessex' but he also wrote many poems describing its countryside. For much of his life he was unhappy and this shows in his writing – but his later poems are full of beauty.

Gerard Manley Hopkins (1844–89) was a Roman Catholic priest. His poems are remarkable for their rhythm and the way he uses words to create a kind of music. None of the poems were published while he was alive: they were first collected and published by the poet (and his friend) Robert Bridges.

William Ernest Henley (1849–1903) is usually known as W.E. Henley and edited various magazines and a dictionary of slang words. He published several collections of poems and was a friend of Robert Louis Stevenson.

Robert Louis Stevenson (1850–94) was a Scotsman, born in Edinburgh. As a child, he was often ill but when he grew up, he travelled abroad to escape the damp and cold Scottish climate. He is famous for his adventure novels *Treasure Island* and *Kidnapped,* and also for the spooky story *The Strange Case of Dr Jekyll and Mr Hyde*.

Ella Wheeler Wilcox (1850–1919) was an American journalist and poet and was once described as 'the most popular poet of either sex and of any age'. Her poems are romantic and full of hope about how good life can be. In recent times, however, her writing has fallen out of fashion.

Henry van Dyke (1852–1933) was a pastor in the Presbyterian Church in New York City and later a professor of English literature. He wrote a number of hymns and several stories such as 'The First Christmas Tree' which he originally read aloud as sermons. When they were published, he became a very popular writer. During World War One he acted as American minister (or ambassador) to the Netherlands. His poems were published in 1920.

Francis Thompson (1859–1907) lived a life of ill-health and poverty and became addicted to drugs. He was rescued by friends who helped him break his drug habit and encouraged him to write poetry. His poems show how God is present in the everyday world.

Edward Thomas (1878–1917) did not start writing poetry until he was over thirty. Almost all his poems are about the English countryside and were written before World War One changed so many things. Once the war began, he joined the Army and was killed while fighting in Flanders.

Wilfred Owen (1893–1918) was already a poet when the war began in 1914. He joined the Army in 1915 and then his poems began to reflect the true horror of the battlefield. He was shot dead just one week before the war ended. His poems showed people that war was not glorious and fun but was a cruel and terrible waste of life.

Index of First Lines

93

Index of Poets